TO MY LOVE
(for whom I searched for ages and lives)

WITH LOVE

FOR LOVE

FROM LOVE

Books on Sri Sathya Sai Baba and Sri Shirdi Sai Baba

Satya Sai Avatar: Glimpses of Divinity
R. Mohan Rai
ISBN 81 207 1849 6, 196pp, Rs. 75

Sai Baba: The Source of Light, Love and Bliss
Kailash Kumar & Jorgen Hovgaard
ISBN 81 207 1714 7, 168pp, Rs. 75

Sai Baba: The Rose Fire of Heaven
Krishna Nandan Sinha
ISBN 81 207 1500 4, 192pp, Rs. 85

Sri Sathya Sai Baba: Absolute Sole Lord of Life and Death
Krishna Nandan Sinha
ISBN 81 207 1564 0, 192pp, Rs. 85

Tablets of Truth: Sayings of Sai Baba in a calligraphical script
Andrew Shaw
ISBN 81 207 1665 5, 256pp, Rs. 90

Words of Truth: A Second Compilation of Sayings by Bhagavan Sri Sathya Sai Baba in Calligraphical Script
Andrew Shaw
ISBN 81 207 1905 0, 144pp, Rs. 65

From Where Did You Come? Bhagwan Sri Sathya Sai Baba
Charles P. DiFazio
ISBN 81 207 1928 x, 296pp, Rs. 125

स्वप्न तथा सच्चाईयाँ भगवान के समक्ष
डा॰ नरेश भाटिया
ISBN 81 207 2075 x, 144pp, Rs. 45

Sri Shirdi Sai Baba: The Universal Master
S.P. Ruhela
ISBN 81 207 1664 8, 160pp, Rs. 65

God who Walked on Earth: The Life & Times of Shirdi Sai Baba
Rangaswami Parthasarathy
ISBN 81 207 1809 7, 240pp, Rs. 95

Life History of Shirdi Sai Baba
Ammula Sambasiva Rao
ISBN 81 207 2033 4, 248pp, Rs. 95

Shri Sai Baba
Tr. V.B. Kher
ISBN 81 207 1950 6, 352pp, Rs. 125

Hundred & Eight Names of Shirdi Sai Baba
Vijaya Kumar
ISBN 81 207 2034 2, 120pp, Rs. 50

संत शिरोमणि श्री शिरडी साई बाबा
डा॰ सत्यपाल रुहेला
ISBN 81 207 2073 3, 192pp, Rs. 45

Published by
Sterling Publishers Private Limited

The DREAMS & REALITIES FACE to FACE with GOD

DR. NARESH BHATIA

A Sterling Paperback

STERLING PAPERBACKS
An imprint of
Sterling Publishers (P) Ltd.
L-10, Green Park Extension, New Delhi-110016
Ph.: 6191784, 6191785, 6191023 Fax: 91-11-6190028
E-mail: sterlin.gpvb@axcess.net.in
ghai@nde.vsnl.net.in

The Dreams & Realities, Face to Face with God
©1998, Dr. N.K. Bhatia
ISBN 81 207 2103 9
Reprint 1999

All rights are reserved. No part of this publication may be reproduced, stored in a retrieval system or transmitted, in any form or by any means, mechanical, photocopying, recording or otherwise, without prior written permission of the publisher.

Published by Sterling Publishers Pvt. Ltd., New Delhi-110016.
Printed at Prolific Incorporated, New Delhi-110020.
Cover design by Sterling Studio

CONTENTS

1. The Early Years — 1
2. My Alma Mater — 11
3. Family — 15
4. Trials and Tribulations — 24
5. The Divine Physician — 30
6. Leelas — 47
7. Brother Sham — 64
8. Shakthi — 70
9. Worldly Attachment — 72
10. Sai Ma — 76
11. The Ultimate Truth — 85
12. Free Will — 99
13. Grace — 102
14. Shirdi Sai and Prema Sai — 105
15. The Mission of Sathya Sai — 110
16. Liquid Love — 116
17. Sri Sathya Sai Institute of Higher Medical Sciences — 122
18. Festivals in Prasanthi Nilayam — 151

Afterword — 156

Glossary — 157

Dedication

As I venture to write all that I know about myself—what I have gathered from others and experienced personally—my sincere wish is for all to read about a person for whom the meaning of life has been only LOVE. This LOVE is that which emanates from the depths of the soul and embraces the entire creation. The pleasures and pains that I have faced throughout my life have given me the strength to firmly believe that this LOVE, in its most pure and sublime form, is the very power of God. Hence, I place this humble work of mine with prayers and prostrations at the Divine Lotus Feet of Bhagawan Sri Sathya Sai Baba who is MY LIFE, MY LORD, AND MY LOVE. I pray to my Beloved Swami to give me the strength and wisdom to pen down all that I can recollect about myself for the seekers of Truth to share. I invoke all of His Divine Mercy to flow, enabling me to complete this work, my autobiography, which I offer and dedicate to MY LOVE.

Acknowledgments

My humble prostrations at the Divine Lotus Feet of my Beloved Lord, Bhagawan Sri Sathya Sai Baba, who gave me this physical frame and the experiences of LOVE and LIFE.

I offer my heartfelt gratitude to my revered parents, Mrs. and Professor C.L. Bhatia, who brought me on this Earth and nurtured me with their care and sacrifice.

I also convey my loving thanks to my wife, Poonam, and our two daughters, Shweta and Rachita, for the blissful family life that we live.

To all my relatives and friends, especially those whose names and experiences appear in this book, I am obliged for all the warmth that they have shared with me.

A special thank you to my loving brother Sham and his wife, Usha Bhabi, for the affection they have extended to me.

I would like to thank Mrs. and Mr. K. Chakravarthi, I.A.S., Registrar of Sri Sathya Sai Institute of Higher Learning, for reading the manuscript of this work and offering their valuable advice and encouragement.

I also thank Mrs. Amita Shenoi for her help in designing the cover.

My sincere thanks go to Mr. Vijay C. Amin, for his help in reading the copy for content and in making the text ready for print. I shall always remain indebted to brother Dr. Ramesh Wadhwani and Sunita Bhabi for all that they have done for me and my family.

I am extremely grateful to brother Hetal Damania of M/s. Sai Mudra for getting this book printed and published with such loving care.

I extend my soul-felt and deepest thanks to Mrs. Reshma, whom Bhagawan Baba sent as His Divine instrument for editing this text. Without her many hours of labor and strenuous work, my dreams would have remained only dreams, and never become the reality that you hold in your hands.

Finally, I thank you, dear readers, for allowing me to share with you this Nectar Divine, my experiences **FACE TO FACE WITH GOD.**

Dr. N. K. Bhatia

November 23, 1993

Chapter 1

The Early Years

In the early morning hours of September 27, 1951, I emerged from my revered mother's womb, welcomed by the first rays of sun on this most beautiful planet that God created and to which He Himself descended on so many occasions. My birth as a son was not welcomed since there were already four brothers elder to me in our family. My father, Late Professor C.L. Bhatia of the Government College, Ludhiana in Punjab left for work a little disturbed as he greatly desired a daughter. From birth, God Almighty has been extremely kind to me; a full half hour after me, my twin sister, Meenakshi was born. Upon receiving the joyous news, my father literally danced in his classroom.

My mother took great pains in bringing up all three of us—in addition to my sister and me, the brother just elder to me, Rakshit, was hardly two years old at the time of my birth. Another interesting feature of this date, September 27th, is that another elder brother of mine, Santosh, also opened his eyes on the same date five years earlier.

In my mother's lap and in the cradle, life began moving, and I started taking tiny steps to measure the miles and miles of the journey of life that lay ahead. My mother poured into my ears the loving stories of Rama, Krishna, and other gods and goddesses. A special lullaby that my mother used to sing, "Karuna Kanja Ramya Rave" described the glorious tale of Lord Rama. To this day, I sing this lullaby to young children.

At the age of two or three years, I first felt the power, strength, mercy, and presence of God. On the auspicious festival of Janmashtami, Lord Krishna's birthday, my mother would make wonderful sweets and delicacies. I loved those dishes so much, that I learned how to prepare them myself, and I make them every year in my own home. Yet, on this first Janamashtami that I remember, I kept fast for the entire day and never felt hungry. I felt as if Krishna, my loving companion of Dwaraka, had himself been feeding me milk, curds, and butter all day long. Although I had not eaten a single morsel, my stomach felt absolutely full. At midnight, the cucumber offered as *prasad* transformed into sweet on its own. This miracle continues in our home year after year. At the tender age of three, Krishna, my personal God, imprinted Himself on my heart.

I began attending school at the age of four. Even at a young age, I loved everyone: teachers, family members, friends. I used to accompany my father in performing social service; with a tiny hand I would lift earth, sand, bricks (half at a time), to help in the construction of an Open Air Theater at the Government College, Ludhiana. At that time, the seed of *seva* was sown in my heart, and as it grew, I would incessantly search for the opportunity to be of some service to someone.

At the Government Model High School, Ludhiana, I was fortunate enough to be taught by a very noble group of teachers. Under them, I learned my first lessons of knowledge. I remember reading the stories of many great leaders and being inspired to emulate their heroic deeds. I, too, would become Bhagat Singh; I would also be a lover of our beloved motherland; I would face death for Her sake. The last lines of the story of Socrates reverberated in my mind: "The world gives a cup of poison to Socrates and then raises statues in his memory."

With this, I began to realize my path, my goal, my aim....I have to love my motherland Bharat, the greatest land on Earth. I must live a life of sacrifice, a life of purity, a life of goodness. The philosopher in me craved to gaze at the stars all throughout the night. I would go out into the drizzling rain and feel the cool water splashing on my face. In the vastness of nature I searched for something, something, something. That something was LOVE. Could there be a human embodiment of LOVE? If so, how would that person look? Would I ever touch that being, talk to that great Self? The answers to all of these questions were kept for me in the stores of time.

The saplings of religion and spirituality began to grow in me, and I would sit and pray for hours together in the shrine of our home. Reading the Holy *Geeta* and trying to understand its meaning became a part of my daily routine. Krishna was my charioteer, and I surrendered myself completely to Him as my Master.

During my schooldays, I used to participate in many dramas and extra-curricular activities. Often, I was the only boy selected to dance with the group of girls. My father would take us to National Cadet Corps (N.C.C.) camps; we also acted in the cultural programs of the college. Once, when my father was away in Jammu and Kashmir to conduct exams, my mother fell ill. My eldest brother, Basant *Bhayya* took charge of all the household chores, and the rest of us helped him. It was then that I learned personal responsibility and self-reliance.

One day my grandfather became very sick with diarrhea. My mother washed sets and sets of sheets as they became spoiled. That was the first time that I became interested in serving suffering humanity. As I look back on my life now, I feel great satisfaction in knowing that God, in His Infinite Mercy, bestowed on me these hands that have served hundreds and hundreds of suffering brethren. These very hands have washed their stools, urine, and made me feel elevated in my own self with peace and love.

I do not remember telling many lies in my childhood, but one situation I remember in particular detail. When I was in the fifth standard, I was bitten by a female monkey when I tried to force her to eat a piece of ginger. That day in class I had learned a maxim which said that monkeys cannot recognize the taste of ginger because they have never eaten it. I thought that if I made a monkey taste it, I could prove the maxim wrong. And in my attempt, I was badly bitten by the monkey. Arriving home in tears, I told my father that I had been bitten by a dog. Immediately, my eldest brother rushed me to our family doctor who quickly administered some injections and bandaged my hand. When we returned home, my father took me in his lap and asked me to tell the truth. I remember receiving my earliest slaps from him, and I confessed the truth. **I learned that one has to pay the price for lying. Truth became my friend.** However, on many occasions, I broke that friendship, only to repent later and to pray to God for His forgiveness. I would ask my Krishna: "Won't you love me even if I am a sinner?" And my Beloved Krishna would run to me, hug me, and accept me time and again. He alone had to help me with my transformation. I am confident that this process will continue until I am completely purified.

In 1961, my two eldest brothers, Basant *Bhayya* and Lalit *Bhayya,* were selected for the Indian Army, and they left for training. My heart acutely felt the sorrow of the separation. I remember expressing my sadness in my first letter to them. "*Bhayya,* I feel as if someone has plucked two beautiful roses from our garden where the rest of the buds have not yet bloomed." The writer in me had arisen and made me compose songs, create poetry, and develop prose. At these times, I would feel as if someone—someone who has been with me for the past several lives—was sitting in the depths of my heart giving me strength and encouragement. The expressions of my inner self continued unfolding themselves in one form or another.

In July, 1962, my father was transferred to the sacred land of Kurukshetra. During our eight-year-stay there, I lost my childhood and entered adolescence. I was admitted to Srimad Bhagavad *Geeta* High School, and there my personality was shaped and molded. I organized many functions and programs. I became the secretary of the school *Bal Sabha*. At that time, I caught the first glimpses of jealousy among friends, and I saw the destruction to which it led. But my eyes were fixed on some higher target, some unseen goal that made me continue on my path with utmost steadfastness.

I distinctly remember the happy day when our Matric (tenth standard) results were announced, and I found my name in the Merit list with a scholarship. During those days, I had a friend, a bit older than me, who was a professional actor. He wanted me to join him on the cinema screen. However, that life had never appealed to me. The same being was supporting me from within, and I continued searching for the physical manifestation of that person.

I took admission in pre-university (medical group) and grew close to one and all. While my extra-curricular activities continued at an even faster pace, I left no stone unturned in the academic arena. In pre-university, we traveled on field trips to various religious places. One of those frequent excursions was to Jyotisar, the holy place where Lord Krishna actually delivered the nectar Divine—the Holy *Geeta*—to Arjuna, making Arjuna His instrument. This Immortal Message was bestowed on all mankind for ages to come. There still exists a banyan tree which is believed to be an offshoot of the original tree under which the Lord delivered His Holy message. Under that tree there are two Lotus Feet carved in marble, marking the place where the Lord stood. There I would lose myself, kissing those feet and washing them with my tears. I believed those feet to be the real ones, of flesh and blood. Like the *gopikas*, waves of love arose in my young heart, and I would imagine my Krishna coming and holding me in His Divine arms. He was everything to me.

Final exams arrived, and I faced them with courage. God's grace allowed me to see another joyous day in my life: I stood first in the pre-university (medical group). The honors showered upon me strengthened my resolve to continue on my chosen path. I became very close with my fellow classmates. Since I called every girl my *didi*, the boys often teased me, calling me "International Brother of Students". Oblivious of what was going on around me, I continued on my journey with Krishna as the only companion in my heart.

Abruptly, in 1967, a period of miseries began. I started experiencing a very strange dream that would make me wake up in the middle of night screaming and sweating profusely. Unable to comprehend what was happening, I would become lost in my inner self. The personification of purity and compassion, with an angelic face, would appear asking me to accompany that Divine Person to a most wonderful place. This someone had been with me for the past several ages and lives, coming with beautiful, marble-white hands and pulling me along. This recurrent dream left me bewildered and dazed every time, and the confusion that it created in my mind began affecting both my health and my emotional stability. Unable to share my innermost thoughts with anyone, I would cry out to my Lord Krishna for guidance. As the days turned into months, my inner agony grew unabated, breaking my concentration in studies as well.

An extremely strange occurrence in December, 1967 brought about my first experience with the **magnitude** of truth. One day, I returned home for lunch and found a *sadhu* at our door. He was speaking to my mother, and on seeing me, he said: "Ma! This son of yours will go to the heights. He will be the luckiest among all your children." Impatient and hungry for lunch, I told the *sadhu* to leave because he would not receive anything from us. Angrily,

I turned to my mother and asked her to get rid of him and to prepare my lunch since I had to return to college soon.

Mother went in, and the man called me. He said: "I know you are having a strange problem; I will solve it." I said: "No, I do not have any problem." He questioned me: "Are you often getting a dream which disturbs you very much?" Imagine my plight! Even today, the details of that scene are meticulously imprinted on my mind. I am standing on the lawn of our house, No. D-35, Kurukshetra University, drenched with perspiration. Mercifully, the *sadhu* looked at me and described every aspect of that loving person of my dream. He went on, not only to predict the future course of events in my life, but also to describe the people that would come and shape my life. One of the things he foretold was that I would not be able to join the Bachelor of Medicine, Bachelor of Surgery (M.B.B.S.) program that year, but I would have to wait for two more years. At that particular time in my life, I was so confident of my abilities, that I proudly told him: "Even if God comes on Earth, He cannot stop my admission to M.B.B.S." The *sadhu* smiled and said: *"Beta!* God is already moving on Earth in human form." Angrily, I replied: "Tell me where He is! I will catch hold of Him and tell Him that He has made a mess of the world. I will cut Him into slices and sections and examine Him under a microscope. Where is He? Where is God?" The *sadhu* responded: "God has taken birth in south India, and you will be **FACE TO FACE WITH HIM ON YOUR 30TH BIRTHDAY."**

How could my young mind of sixteen accept all this? How could my Krishna return to this grief-stricken world? Even if He were to come back, how would He appear? I could not accept any form other than that of my Krishna. The *sadhu's* remaining predictions were as follows:

1. My father would get promoted and leave for the next place from where I would go for the M.B.B.S. program after two years.

2. I would get married as a student.

   3. At the age of 39, my professional career would suddenly change.

   4. After that, no more heights would be attained in worldly matters.

   5. Someone will come into my life and bring a dramatic change. **Each and every prophecy has proved true so far.**

In January, 1968 I was admitted to Post Graduate Institute of Medical Sciences (P.G.I.) Chandigarh for treatment of acute pancreatitis. My stay there for about twenty-five days gave me some insight into the profession that I was planning to enter. Although I was eventually discharged, the pain in my abdomen continued for several months. Consequently, I performed poorly in the final exam, and my dreams for entering medical college were shattered. Distressed in mind and heart, I resigned myself to Krishna and accepted my fate. The first of that *sadhu's* prophecies came true. **Life had taught me yet another lesson—to never feel proud of one's intelligence.** My only recourse was to join the Bachelor of Science (B.Sc.) program and wait for events to unfold.

Scarcely could I understand that my abdominal pains would worsen and remain incurable. On the 8th of November 1968, I woke up early in the morning with something filling my mouth. Immediately, I rushed to the washbasin and spit out a large gush of blood, followed by more bouts of blood. I screamed and promptly fainted. My mother rushed to my side and found me semiconscious. The doctor was summoned. Upon finding me in a state of shock, the physician administered some emergency injections and started a glucose drip. Since she was unable to control the bleeding from my nostrils, the doctor recommended that I be moved to the hospital. Death

"Why fear when I am near"
"Abhaya Hasta - The Divine Hand
that can turn sky into earth and earth into sky"

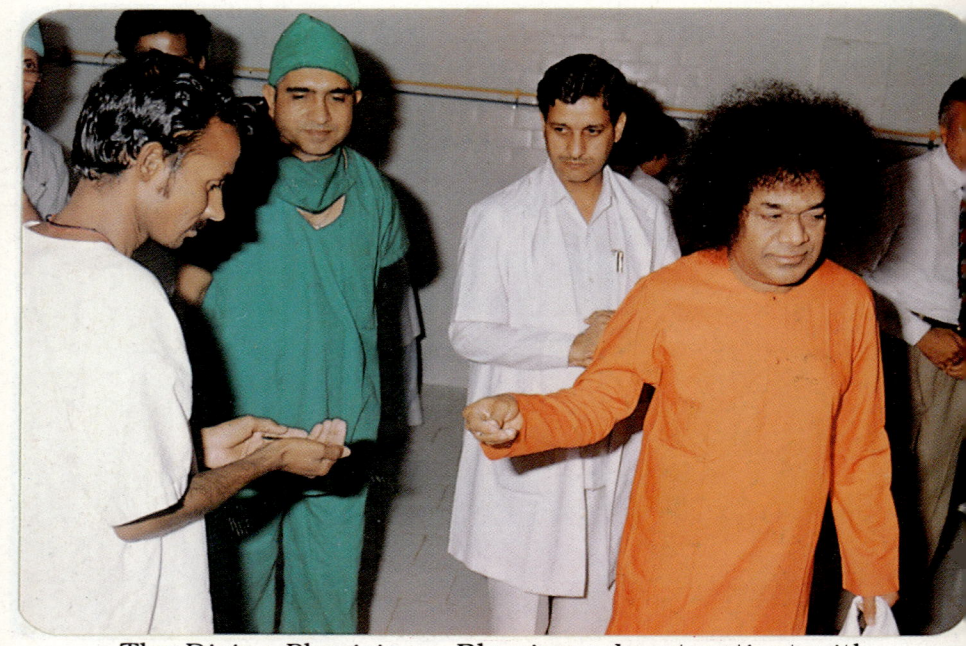

The Divine Physician - Blessing a heart patient with Holy Vibhuti in Cardiology ward.

Swami with Dr. (Mrs.) Poonam Bhatia after inaugurating the New Dental Unit at Sri Sathya Sai General Hospital, Prasanthi Nilayam

was written on my face. Madly my mother rushed to our shrine and fell at Krishna's feet, fervently praying for God to take her life and to spare her son's. She started reading the Holy *Geeta* with all maternal force. The moment she finished reading the *Geeta*—all eighteen chapters—the doctor entered and gave me nasal packings. The unseen hand of Krishna, my savior and my friend, pulled me out of the jaws of death and gave me another lease of life. Krishna manifested His presence by holding my hand when I could not even move it on my own. He remained with me until I was declared out of danger, and my condition began to improve. The next day my father brought his promotion and transfer orders to Sangrur (Govt. Ranbir college). He was asked to move immediately. Yet another prediction—that my father would move and from there I would join the M.B.B.S. program—proved true.

Because my elder brothers were involved in their higher studies, only my sister Meenakshi, my youngest brother Alok, and I were moved to Sangrur. I joined in the second year of the B.Sc. program there, but to my utter dismay there was a big problem regarding the syllabi. The curricula of the courses covered in Sangrur were different, and I had to struggle day in and day out just to survive at my studies.

My father was the one to announce our results. When my name came up, he scolded me publicly saying: "You want to become a doctor! You cannot even become a compounder." Those words pierced my heart, and my inner being arose from its slumber. I plunged myself into my studies with such great intensity that I was not even aware when the day dawned or when the night fell.

I cannot describe the jubilation that I felt when the results of B.Sc. were announced. This son of God broke all previous records and was placed First on Merit in the entire University. Congratulations poured in from all directions, and I remember feeling as if I were six inches taller that day. There are no shortcuts to success, and hard work always ensures one's reward. The following five "W"s were my constant companions:

> **W**ishing
> **W**illing
> **W**orking
> **W**aiting
> **W**inning

I had won the game, and was given the prestigious "Roll of Honor Award." Tears of gratitude rolled down my face as I touched the feet of my revered parents and teachers. Their efforts and prayers made us see that day.

> hildren must grow up in an atmosphere of reverence, devotion, mutual service and cooperation. They must be taught respect for parents, teachers and elders. Children must grow in the awareness of the brotherhood of man and fatherhood of God.
>
> *"Sathya Sai"*

CHAPTER 2

MY ALMA MATER

In July, 1970 I joined the M.B.B.S. program in one of the most prestigious medical colleges in India: Medical College, Amritsar. During my first professional year, in December, 1971, India and Pakistan went to war. As medical students, we formed groups to go to our brethren soldiers and serve them.

My love for Krishna grew tremendously during that year. On my wall hung a beautiful photograph of my beloved Krishna, and I would talk to Him for hours on end. His loving eyes conveyed so much to me. Days went on passing in this bliss. Then, one day, a bolt from the blue shocked us all. In college, we had a teacher accustomed to harassing and exploiting students. When the situation reached its breaking point, we students decided to take matters into our own hands and force him to leave. This unfortunate episode taught me many things. I realized the great power of Truth and the strength that comes to you when you follow it. I also experienced the supreme peace that develops when you are submerged in your own Self.

My second professional year brought me close to many people who left indelible imprints on my mind. One of them was our revered college principal, Dr. Mohinder Singh Grewal, an institution in himself. The others include: Dr. J.L. Bhatia, Professor and Head of the Department of Chest Diseases and Tuberculosis, a godfather to me, and Dr.(Mrs.) Saroj Sanan, Professor of Pharmacology, from whom I received a mother's love as well as a teacher's spiritual guidance. She was a follower of one of the greatest seers of modern times, Maharshi Yogiraj Sri Aurobindo. We would sit together for hours meditating and praying. Sri Aurobindo's life along with that of The Mother made me go deeper into the realms of supra consciousness from where I could see through time and space. Before my spiritual progress advanced too quickly for my own good, Madam Sanan stopped me. As I slowed down, I felt a sea of change within me. I realized then that I must live the life of a spiritual *sadhaka* and spread the message of LOVE to the world. I used to speak on occasion to friends about higher values, integrated consciousness, pure love, service, and many other things. These blissful days added charm to my physical body, mental makeup, psyche, and spirit.

How can I forget Dr. Rissam Harbhajan Singh? One year senior to me, he was a person with a crystal clear sense of Self. I remember how the two of us would sit together all night watching the moon move across the sky, casting its rays through the leaves of a huge banyan tree. That tree became symbolic of my life: I would become morally upright and steadfast in my faith like the trunk of that tree. Like the limbs and leaves I would reach out to people in other places through love and service. During these days Mother Nature taught me many lessons. God has given His power in the form of Nature to bestow health, wealth and prosperity on His children. We should never harm Her with our greed.

Rissam *Bhayya* was the secretary of our college Literary Forum, and I had the privilege of serving as joint secretary, subsequently becoming secretary and then being made Life Advisor. The Literary Forum, which included all extra-curricular activities and cultural events of the college, revealed many hidden talents. People around me wondered how one person could do so much. But I always felt someone pushing me from within.

I threw myself into all types of activities of the college—cultural, academic and athletic. Outside the college, I engaged myself in social service as well, traveling to villages and undertaking health care activities. Loving the poorest of the poor and envisioning God in them allowed me to develop an overwhelming sense of expansion for all mankind. I felt like loving everything and everyone in creation.

One rivulet of the giant river of love flowing in me developed for one of my collegemates. Two years younger than me, he was the son of one of my previous professors. When his parents came to admit him in medical college, they entrusted him to me and requested me to treat him as my younger brother. Truly, that was the love that I always extended to him. Coincidentally, he physically looked like me, so many people thought we were biological brothers. Unable to resist the temptations of adolescence, my friend indulged in several unsavory habits. My attempts to help him change his ways only served to push him away from me. Our differences grew to such an extent that our friendship completely broke. Having been so attached to him, I could not bear the loss. I became an emotional wreck and ultimately decided to end my life.

I wanted to electrocute myself, but the moment I switched on the button, the electricity went off. I thought of burning myself but failed in that attempt also. I then decided to hang myself and took hold of my leather belt, tied it around my neck, and jumped. The belt broke. I found someone slapping me hard saying: "You are destined to live and work for Me—don't be a fool. You cannot die." There was not a single soul to be seen. Rationality poured back in me, and I decided to live and face life with courage. I realized how a man gets entrapped in his own foolish creations and makes mistakes. But what **God destines, happens.**

I often had to travel between college in Amritsar and my home in Sangrur. On one such trip, I happened to pick up a book entitled <u>Man of Miracles</u>, by Howard Murphet at the book stall. On the cover was a picture of an Indian man with long curly hair. The bookstall owner told me to read about Sai Baba who claims to be an incarnation of God. I laughed out loud, scoffing at the owner, but curiosity got the better of me, and I left the shop a few minutes later, book in hand.

As the bus started, I began to read and quickly grew perplexed when I read that this man refers to himself as being Rama, Krishna, and all other previous incarnations of God. His last birth was as Shirdi Sai Baba. I could not accept the fact that my Krishna was living and moving on this Earth in human form. By the time I reached Sangrur six hours later, I had read about two hundred pages of the book. I felt some strange sensations within myself. Unable to decide what to do about this man, I handed myself over to the will of MY LOVE, the LOVE that had always supported me in my hours of tests and turmoils, the LOVE that followed me everywhere like my own shadow, the LOVE that always sang for me, the LOVE that constantly gave me strength and encouragement. I withdrew within and began contemplating as to whether Bhagawan Sri Sathya Sai Baba could really be my Krishna. A sense of peace and tranquilllity came over me when I thought about Baba, but it would be many years and many tests before I accepted Him as **everything in my life.**

> Schooling is not merely for *Ahara* and *Ananda*, earning a living and learning to enjoy leisure. If is to activate the divine qualities of *Viveka, Vairagya* and *Vichakshana*, to ensure in the individual the stabilising virtues of *Shanthi, Sathya* and *Dharma* through the blossoming of *Prema*.
>
> **"Sathya Sai"**

Chapter 3

Family

Although I sincerely believe that we are all part of the Divine family, and I cultivate those feelings of love and regard for all with whom I come in contact, here I must narrate a few incidents about my God-given, immediate family—my wife Poonam, and my two daughters Shweta and Rachita. I say God-given because all three of them are truly gifts from God. Swami has permeated each and every aspect of my family life right from my marriage onwards.

The first week of March, 1974 was a tumultuous time in our medical college. Despite the atmosphere of chaos and gloom that prevailed due to an unspeakable crime that took place, I remained as calm as the eye of the storm. Amidst all this, I saw her. An orange robe appeared before my eyes and directed me: *"She is for you"*. As I had already been introduced to Sai Baba by this time, I obeyed His orders implicitly. On the 8th of July 1974, I received dearest Poonam as my wife. And one more prophecy of that *sadhu* came true as "I got married while still a student"—a situation that I could have never imagined previously. The suddenness of my wedding naturally caused some uneasy feelings in my family, but my firm resolution to have Poonam never wavered.

The day for which every man dreams, dawned for me on September 12, 1975. At exactly 4.15.08 p.m., the cry of a most beautiful doll made the doors of heaven open upon me. She was to call me "Papa." When I gave her the maiden kiss of her life, tears of gratitude and joy rolled down my cheeks. As the happy news spread, I received hearty congratulations from all sides. One of the most cherished blessings I received was from my godmother, Madam Sanan. She told me: "Naresh, I have become a grandmother today; purity has come to your house; name her *Shweta*." Accordingly, our daughter was named. The distance that had developed between my parents and us slowly diminished, and their visits to their granddaughter marked the culmination of our period of emotional and physical separation.

In April, 1976, Poonam received her posting as dental surgeon in Civil Hospital, Abohar, while I was still completing my residency or house job in Amritsar. I could not leave Amritsar nor did Poonam want to miss her opportunity in Abohar. Ultimately, I had to bear the pangs of separation from my wife and darling daughter for the next one-and-a-half years. It was not until September 29th, 1977, that I was reunited with my family when I, too, was posted in Abohar as medical officer at the E.S.I. dispensary. One of my cherished goals in life was fulfilled on that day—I began practicing as a full-fledged doctor to love and serve mankind.

While working in Abohar, I received a most unique opportunity. The Iron Lady of India, the late Mrs. Indira Gandhi, suddenly fell sick while visiting our area, and I was fortunate enough to be called to attend on her. I had the privilege of eating breakfast with her and got her autograph on my letter pad. Never have I come across such a gracious lady with the aristocratic charm that she possessed.

January 3, 1980 is another day I will never forget. A thick fog covered the entire area, and at about 8 a.m., we received the message that there had been a terrible accident involving a car and a bus. One person died instantly, and two were in critical condition. I was preparing to leave in ambulance when the bus carrying the casualties came in. All of us were stunned to learn the identity of the victims: one was Mr. Sajjan Jakhar, son of Choudhury Balram Jakhar who was running in the forthcoming elections. (The Janta Party Government had fallen, and Lok Sabha elections were to be held on January 5th.) Mr. Sajjan's neck area from head to chest was completely crushed—not a single bone remained intact. The other victim was the brother-in-law of Mr. Sajjan and a very close friend of mine, Mr. Rai Singh Kaswan.

We rushed Mr. Sajjan into the operation theater and started resuscitation. A team of doctors from the Army Hospital and several local specialists were also present. All our efforts to revive him failed. With hand gestures, my former Senior Medical Officer asked me about the patient's condition. I conveyed that his pulse and heartbeat were absent; respiration had ceased; pupils were dilated and non-reactive. He walked out with tears in his eyes, and I heard him crying outside. Some force within propelled me to pray to Baba to save this noble son of our area. Even his opponents had always respected his humble and honorable nature. He always loved me like an elder brother. If he were to die, we would all suffer a great loss.

After injecting drugs into his heart and starting a cardiac massage, we struggled for several minutes giving him artificial breathing. To our utter amazement, his heart began beating on its own. We put him on an intermittent positive pressure respirator that was manually operated, and continued praying for him. His blood pressure and pulse returned, and we made plans to move him to Christian Medical College, Ludhiana for treatment of his serious head injury. Since the weather was so foggy, no helicopter could land, and we had to depend on the road route to cover a distance of about 240 kilometers.

We began the journey, but after about 40 kilometers, the I.P.P. respirator got jammed. There was no alternative but for me to give him mouth-to-mouth resuscitation for the remainder of the journey—about 4 1/2 hours. Only Baba could have given me the strength to reach Ludhiana safely. Mr. Sajjan's father had already reached the hospital and was awaiting our arrival. The head of the department said to him: "Thank this young doctor who bravely brought your son here." As the towering (6'6") Choudhury Balram Jakhar Ji embraced me, there were tears in both of our eyes. I told him: "Sir, it is not me, but my Bhagawan who has brought him here. You will see, you will be the next Speaker of the Lok Sabha, and Mr. Sajjan will be the next Member of Legislative Assembly (M.L.A.) from Abohar." Elections for the Lok Sabha had not yet taken place, and the ones for the Punjab assembly were nowhere near ready to be held. But some force prompted me to make this declaration.

Believe it or not, the statement proved 100% true. Choudhury Balram Jakhar won the election with one of the widest margins of victory. He was elected Speaker and held that post for the next ten years. His son, Mr. Sajjan, recovered after a six-month hospital stay and became the next M.L.A. from Abohar in the elections held in 1981. The love of that family continues to be very dear to my heart. Mr. Sajjan is now a minister in Punjab, and his father was our Central Agriculture Minister. Choudhury Sahib has been to Prasanthi Nilayam and received Swami's blessings.

As both my wife and I became busy with our respective jobs in Abohar and with our darling daughter, time flew by in its accustomed manner. During the summer of 1980, Poonam conceived our next child, and my one and only thought at that time was caring for her. I wanted to ensure her happiness and well-being during pregnancy. After our most precious second daughter, Rachita, was born on February 27, 1981, Poonam and the girls went to my in-laws' home for a few months.

I had been conducting an honorary class for homoeopathic students during those days. With my family away, I had more free time to spend with my students. Eight of them, four boys and four girls, would come to my house, and I would teach them for hours. All of them were very bright and courteous students. Since I was alone, they helped me with cooking and keeping house; they became a small family for me. Two sisters among them were particularly close to me. One day, as the younger of the two was talking to me, I abruptly asked her if she had a heart problem. She surprisingly replied that, in fact, she had a hole in her heart and often suffered from breathlessness and other symptoms. I had not seen any of these, but something from within prompted me to question her. I instructed her to have faith in Krishna and to read one chapter of the Holy *Geeta* everyday. As I read the *Geeta* daily, I invited them to come and listen. Within one month the girl's condition started improving, and she became perfectly healthy. God, in His Infinite Mercy, cured that lovely child.

I had been suffering from hyperacidity and a peptic ulcer which gave me severe abdominal pain. My students were the only ones present to take care of me. Once the bouts of bleeding from my mouth were so extreme that my students contacted my wife. I did not want to trouble Poonam because she already had two small girls to look after. However, she came and remained with me until I felt better. During this time, Abohar was in the grip of dengue fever, and I, too, fell prey to it. My temperature shot up to 106.5°F and I became delirious. My students again contacted my wife. When she arrived, I was already under the effect of some heavy drugs and was completely disoriented. Severe cardiac arrhythmias and fluctuating blood pressure ensued. I found myself in the depths of despair both mentally and physically. No one could understand the trauma that I was undergoing.

The Lord Himself confirmed and blessed our marriage. In our very first interview, on September 21, 1981, the first thing Swami asked when we entered was: "Doctor, what is the news?" As this was our first physical contact with Swami, I was surprised as to how he knew that I was a doctor. I replied, "All fine." He asked me: "Who told you to marry her? It was Swami's directive." I was reminded of the orange robe and Swami's words at that time: *"She is for you."* He continued: **"I know your past, present, and future. I know the past, present, and future of everyone."** Baba then placed one hand on each of our heads and said: "Go and live a very happy, long life."

Since this was our first trip to Puttaparthi, we went to see some of the sites. One of the most important was Swami's birthplace, at which a Shiva temple was built. I sat, engrossed in the beauty of the statue of Shiva (which happens to be installed exactly at the place where the child was laid on the floor. Rachita, who was only about seven months old at the time, was sitting in my lap. Seeing a banana placed on the altar, she made gestures indicating that she wanted that banana. I asked the priest if Rachita could have it, and he flatly refused. I tried to pacify my daughter, but to no avail; the more I tried to calm her, the more she cried. In my heart, I prayed to Bhagawan: a small, innocent child wants Your *prasad*. Does it matter if You eat it or if she eats it? As I was praying, the garland around Lord Shiva's head swirled in a circular motion and broke in two, flying through the air to land on us. The priest interpreted this as a Divine signal to bless the girl with the banana, and he offered it to us.

In July, 1982, we made our next journey to Bhagawan's Lotus Feet. On the way to Puttaparthi, we stopped in Hyderabad to see Shivam temple. Dr. Ashok Gupta, one of my colleagues, and his family were accompanying us on this trip. The temple doors were closed, but on our sincere and persistent requests, the caretaker agreed to open them for us. As he opened the doors, we saw a beautiful photograph of Swami on the opposite wall. The moment we stepped inside, Rachita started rolling on the floor, uttering: "Baba, Baba, Baba..." She continued moving all over the floor for about forty minutes as if in a trance. As she was only 1 1/2 years old, Rachita had not started speaking yet. We took this incident as the moment when Swami gave her the gift of speech. The caretaker told us that Rachita must be some very noble soul who had been born in our family. I agreed with him for Swami had blessed Rachita immensely on our last trip. Young children, for whom the harsh realities of the external world have not begun, remain engrossed in the serene realities of the Divine.

Our wedding anniversary was approaching, and I was confident that Swami would call us on that day. I mentioned this several times to Dr. Gupta. On the morning of July 8, 1982, our anniversary, Swami did not come anywhere near us in *darshan*. Dr. Gupta chided me: "Where is your faith in Swami, now?" I replied: "Sir, evening *darshan* is yet to come," so firm was my belief. In the evening, Swami skipped the gents' side altogether. Again, Dr. Gupta teased: "Now, what?" I cried out to Swami inside: Swami, You say that all ladies are Your daughters, and they have come to their Mother's home. If Poonam is Your daughter, I happen to be Your son-in-law. Is this the traditional Indian way to welcome a son-in-law home on such an auspicious occasion as his wedding anniversary? At that very moment, Swami turned back, walked directly toward me and from a distance, motioned to me, saying: "Wedding anniversary. Come." I happily stood up and said to Dr. Gupta: "This is faith." Upon seeing me walk to the verandah, Poonam and Rachita joined me. Shweta was nowhere to be found. Dr. Gupta's daughter, who was sitting with Poonam, came with them instead. In the verandah, Swami asked: "Who is she?", pointing at Dr. Gupta's daughter. I replied: "Swami, friend's daughter." He repeated: "Friend's daughter." Swami asked me: "Where is your elder daughter?" I answered: "Swami, I do not know." In my heart, I was feeling sad that Shweta would be missing this golden opportunity. Suddenly, Swami pointed: "She is coming." Shweta nearly ran to us, with tears streaming down her face.

We entered the interview room, and Swami talked about certain spiritual matters. When it was our turn to enter the inner interview room, I stood to one side in order to allow my wife and daughters to enter first. Swami commented: "Gracious." Swami informed those waiting in the outer interview room: "They have their marriage anniversary today." Coming in to us, He again said: "Marriage anniversary." I said: "Yes, Swami." The Divine Father and Mother, the Ultimate Power, placed His left hand on my head and His right hand on my wife's head and said: "I bless. You have a very happy, long, and prosperous married life." Thrice, he repeated these blessed words. For what more can we ask? God Himself was blessing His children.

Swami truly knows everything about us, even the most minute details of our lives. On December 9, 1983, Sham and I had an amazing interview with Swami. Sham is my dearest and most beloved friend who deserves a chapter to himself. Swami spoke to both of us for nearly 2 hours and 45 minutes. He narrated every small fact of our lives regarding our marriages and married lives. Both of us were stunned as to how meticulously Swami revealed everything. I asked Baba: "Swami, how do you know everything about us?" Swami smiled and began describing the location and layout of our house in Abohar. He said: "In your bedroom, in a particular corner, there is a small table. On that table, there is a lamp and under that lamp there is Swami's photo." He precisely described His pose in that photograph. "In that photo, there is Swami's face and on that face, there are TWO EYES. Those eyes watch and see everything happening there."

There is one very strange mystery regarding my family. During the same trip to Puttaparthi with Sham in December, 1983, we were seated for *darshan* when Swami came to us. He asked me: "Where is son?" I did not know to what or to whom He was referring as I had only two daughters. So I asked: "Swami, what son?" I thought that perhaps Bhagawan was asking about Sham. I pointed toward him and said: "He is there, Baba." But Baba again said: "No, not he. Where is your son?" I was completely confused. Only Swami knew what He was talking about. There was no way for me to solve the mystery.

The next day, again Swami approached me: "Where is your son?" I replied: "Swami, I do not know." He then asked: "Where are your daughters?" I answered: "At Abohar." He asked: "Where?" I said: "Swami, in Punjab at Abohar." "And where is your wife?" My reply: "Swami, at Abohar along with children." With a mischievous grin, Baba asked: "Where is your second wife?" I said: "Swami, no second wife." He moved as if to leave and then turned back: "When are you leaving?" I replied: "Swami, on the fourteenth (of December)." He said: "Oh, the fourteenth." I was praying with all my heart for blessings before we had to leave, and they did come in the form of our long and detailed interview with Bhagawan on December 9th.

For the third consecutive day, Swami asked: "Where is wife?" Again, I replied: "Swami, at Abohar." "No, where is second wife?" "Swami, nowhere." He said: "No, no. She is sitting there (pointing to the ladies side). She has come from America." He smiled, laughed, blessed me, and moved on, creating an ocean of thoughts, flooding my mind with confusion and bewilderment. I earnestly wanted to ask Him: "Bhagawan, what is all this?" I could only appeal to my Lord: Swami, please do not test me anymore; my threshold to weep at Thy Lotus Feet has been surpassed.

Chapter 4

Trials and Tribulations

Life has shown me many good days, but several bad ones as well, many of them relating to my profession and career path. Throughout it all, I have done my best to maintain faith in God, to believe that everything that happens is for the best. In hindsight, I can now see that things had to happen as they did. But, during those hours of desperation, all seemed very bleak. Only Bhagawan imparted to me the strength to undergo my trials and tribulations.

My problems began right in college. The fact that I was delayed from joining the M.B.B.S. program by two years due to acute pancreatitis has already been outlined. Before leaving medical college, I faced another giant hurdle. For the first time in my life, I tasted academic failure. I could not pass my M.B.B.S. final exam in the first attempt. During the practical part of the exam in medicine, my pet subject, the examiner grew irritated with me. I correctly diagnosed the patient as I was supposed to, and I even validated my response by quoting the textbook. However, my answer was not the diagnosis he expected or the one he wanted, and so he gave me very poor marks. The result was that I would have to wait for another six months before retaking the exam. I accepted my fate quietly as Poonam was expecting our first child, and I had to look after her health as well.

While serving as Medical Officer at Civil Hospital Abohar, I had a personal and professional clash with one of my superiors. As a result, I was transferred to the village of Dharangwala on September 27, 1980. Since my reputation in Abohar had become quite esteemed, many people were disturbed when they came to know of my departure. My good friend, Vijinder, in particular, became quite distressed. He became so upset that he vowed he would commit suicide if

Love - The Communication with Sai

Beloved Lord with Dr. Bhatia and his wife and daughters

Brother Sham, Dear Sanjay Chhiber and Dr. Bhatia -
"Smiles of Love and Trust"

I left. In all sincerity, I pacified Vijinder and convinced him that his death was not the answer to my dilemma. Once again, I accepted the will of Sai and started working in the village Dharangwala. I established myself quite nicely in that village and, with the help of the villagers, we changed the face of their dispensary. About eight months later, I shifted back to Abohar.

In December 1981, I received orders of my posting as Demonstrator in the Department of Pathology, Medical College Patiala. Since I had always dreamt of being a surgeon, the field of pathology had never entered my mind. Moreover, I was not keen on leaving Abohar. Poonam, however, convinced me that I must not miss the opportunity to complete my post-graduation in medicine (M.D.), and I should at least try to find out what my prospects were there. Hesitantly, I boarded the bus to Patiala to uncover the future course of events. After visiting Patiala, these were my options:

1. to join Medical College, Patiala, and select pathology as my specialization;
2. to refuse pathology and get debarred for two years before beginning any other specialization;
3. to join an M.S. course in surgery without salary for two to three years.

After weighing the various pros and cons, I selected the first option but not very enthusiastically. Something inside was holding me back: my ego. Time and again I considered the second one, waiting and then trying to specialize in surgery.

On December 21, 1981, my wife had gone to work, and I was lying down on the sofa staring at the blessed photograph of Baba. I was thinking about the career decisions to be made and found myself rather desperate. Tears were brimming in my eyes, and I just placed myself in Swami's hands.

Mercifully, He appeared to me saying: "Why not pathology? Swami has sent you there. So many works you want to do—writing autobiography and then you want to write another book. And then one on the *Geeta* and then on this and that. If you go to surgery, will you have time to write all that you want to write or do? Swami will free you at 2 p.m. everyday and then you can do anything. Go, join pathology."

That was the moment of decision, the directive, the order from Swami. He alone knows what is best for us. I wrote to my sister-in-law to find suitable accommodation for me in Patiala and informed her that I would be in Patiala on December 25th, Christmas Day, to finalize my plans. When my sister-in-law told me she had seen a place, House No. 27, I immediately approved. Two plus seven is the Divine number nine; my birthday is 27th September, the ninth month of the year. Even Swami approved the house because that was the place where He would show us His *leelas*.

I lived quite happily in Patiala until problems with my department began early in 1983. There was a power struggle between two professors. The post-graduate students were fed up with the attitude and actions of one of the professors, and they approached higher authorities for help in saving their careers. The pressure to choose sides grew so great that I finally yielded and joined my colleagues against one of the professors. My career depended on the outcome of this struggle, and it caused me a great deal of mental stress and anxiety. At the same time, our elder daughter developed vitiligo which only added to our worries. Living away from my family did not help matters, so I tried to get my wife transferred from Abohar to Patiala or somewhere nearby. I failed in that attempt and only succeeded in getting her removed even from Abohar. Everything was weighing heavily on my mind.

I learned that there was to be a Bal-Vikas Group III training course in Prasanthi Nilayam, and I wanted to be at the Divine Lotus Feet to receive His blessings. Swami blessed me amply during that trip. I would sit and contemplate on Swami's grandeur, writing volumes of poetry. These verses arose from deep within a yearning soul verbalizing the pangs for the Supreme Soul. I wished for Bhagawan to grant His consent for the publication of these works, and He graciously did so on August 11th and 19th.

Upon returning to Patiala, I discovered that things in the college had gone from bad to worse. Many accusations were made on both sides and, one fine day, I received the news that my candidacy for admission to M.D. was cancelled on very flimsy grounds. I could not believe the news. My appeal to the officer in charge was set aside. All of my dreams and hopes were shattered in one stroke. There was no light at the end of this dark tunnel of miseries—no hope left for me at all. There was no choice but to accept, accept, accept my destiny yet again.

I plunged myself into service activities. At the time, I was posted in the blood bank of Medical College, Patiala. With the grace of Baba, I had endeared myself to nearly everyone with devotion and dedication. I went to various places for organizing voluntary blood donation camps and found it to be one of the most thrilling experiences. I decided to dedicate the rest of my life to the voluntary blood donation movement. My burning heart would receive some solace and new avenues would allow me to channelise my energy into something productive and worthwhile. With Bhagawan's grace, my work expanded and bore fruit, bringing me many awards and achievements. However, I always felt that the best honor one could receive was **the strength** to undertake the next social work. This sort of thinking gave me the courage to continue, but my lack of a post-graduate degree continued to cause me pain somewhere deep inside myself. That which cannot be cured must be endured.

In our December, 1983 interview, Swami asked me about the situation in Punjab. I told Him: "Bhagawan, it is very bad." Swami said: "Yes, yes, it is all dirty politics there." I asked: "Bhagawan, what should Sai devotees do in such circumstances?" Swami frowned at me and replied: "Are there some special Sai devotees? **All those who believe in God and pray are My devotees. I am Sarva Naam Sarva Dev Swaroop. I am the One with every name and every form.**" What a great truth Bhagawan revealed to me.

Then, with great emotional upheaval, I narrated all that had taken place pertaining to my M.D. cancellation. I had put in so much time and hard work for so many years, only to have it taken away in one minute. Swami lovingly took my hand in His and said: "What M.D.? What do you mean by M.D.? M.D. means M.A.D., M.A.D., M A D! All worldly name and fame is only ego, madness, and nothing more. When Swami is there with you, what is the need of M.D.? Don't worry, Swami will take care." Many of my pent-up frustrations got vent on that day. My burden had been taken over by the Lord. As I wept before Swami, He loved me and consoled me.

In May, 1990, tragedy and terror struck Abohar. Thirty people were gunned down by terrorists, and another forty were injured. The tragic episode affected everyone. The Governor of Punjab and several senior government officials rushed to the spot, and the townspeople informed them of many immoral and unethical occurrences in the hospital. The Governor was so distressed that he immediately sent the Secretary of Health and Family Welfare to Abohar to conduct an official inquiry. The minimum punishment he envisaged was a transfer of all the doctors from our hospital. We were allowed to give our station of choice, so that he could adjust us there if possible. As the doctors moved out of the room, I prayed to Swami in all humility: "Baba, you know well with what sincerity I have been working here.

I was working so hard that I could not even come to You for the last three years. Is this justice I receive for doing good work?" I was the last doctor to file out, and I asked the Secretary: "Sir, has there been any complaint filed against me by anyone?" He answered: "No, Dr. Bhatia. In fact, every delegation that has met me has only praised your services." I continued: "Then Sir, why this punishment to me? I don't mind being transferred wherever God wants me to serve His people, but what will incoming doctors think if even Bhatia was thrown out? No one is secure." When I received my transfer orders, I surprisingly found that I was not transferred at all, but I was asked to take over the responsibility of the blood bank in addition to my other duties. The new Chief Medical Officer, Dr. V.K. Bassi, the Surgical Specialist, Dr. V.P. Sethi, and his wife Dr. Sarla Sethi, a renowned Obstetrician and Gynecologist, were all Swami's devotees. Together, we began rebuilding the image of our hospital. During that time, I was fortunate enough to receive many prizes at the district and state levels. I was the only doctor in the state to receive a cash award of Rs. 3,000 from the Governor of Punjab. Earnestly, I thanked Bhagawan for showering His grace on us.

You have to cultivate four types of strength. Strength of body, intellect, discrimination and conduct. Then you become unshakeable; you are on the path of spiritual victory.

"Sathya Sai"

Chapter 5

The Divine Physician

As scientific investigators and inherently rational beings, we find it difficult to explain miracles. Logically, everything that takes place in the human body should have scientific basis. Doctors, especially, like to take credit for curing people and saving lives. More often than not, however, things happen that we simply cannot medically explain. As a doctor myself, I have experienced numerous such miracles firsthand. In these cases, we can only surrender to the mercy of the Divine Physician.

During my house job under Dr. Sanan, I worked extremely hard. There were days when I was the only house surgeon present to take care of almost eighty patients. For days together, I was so busy that I hardly ate or slept. My beard had grown and I could not remember the last time I ate a full meal. One day, a patient by the name of Paramanand Gokul from Mangalore came as an emergency admission to our ward. He had a kidney stone and was in excruciating pain. While examining him, I noticed a triangular aluminum locket around his neck with Swami's face imprinted on it. His X-rays revealed a huge stag horn stone in his kidney. He assured me not to worry as the stone would pass on its own. I laughed incredulously.

Later, he came to my office and asked me if I was Swami's devotee. I replied: "Well, I cannot say that I am Swami's devotee, but I admire Him and believe Him to be some supernatural phenomenon." Mr. Gokul professed to be an ardent follower of Baba. He went on to narrate some of his experiences. He told me that Baba named him and told him that there was a "stone factory" in his body. The stones would form and pass out naturally, without any difficulty. My medical mind refused to accept this explanation. The stone in his kidney was so large that if it passed out naturally, Mr. Gokul's urinary passage would get ripped open. He also told me about his mother's diabetic condition. She had developed pus boils all over her body and found no relief despite several types of treatments. Swami materialized a bowl of *kheer* for her and made her drink it. From that day onwards, her diabetes vanished, and she was completely cured. Another time, Mr. Gokul followed Swami for days together without food or water. Swami called him and snubbed him. Then the Divine Hand produced a half kilogram *khoya*— still hot from the frying pan and asked him to eat it. Mr. Gokul found it extremely awkward to eat in front of Swami. He requested Swami to partake also, but Swami replied: "You take it. I had plenty of milk and milk products during my Krishna Avatar. Now I don't feel like taking such things."

I requested Mr. Gokul to accompany me to my parents' home so that they could also hear his experiences with Swami. I became so enchanted with his locket that I asked him to give it to me. He replied: "Brother, this is Swami's materialized locket, and it is only for me. However, I will do some bhajans and then pray to Swami. If He agrees, I will give it to you." In our home, Mr. Gokul single-handedly sang bhajans for hours, oblivious of the passage of time. I suddenly looked up, and it was almost 10:00 p.m. With his lovely bhajans, he made us all get completely absorbed in Swami's love. After the bhajans, he told me that Swami appeared to him and said: "No, this locket is for you. I will call Dr. Bhatia and give him much better things." Of course, at the time, I did not believe this reply but thought that he did not want to share his locket. However, I did not voice my thoughts.

For the first time in nearly a week I had a delicious home-cooked meal. I was so content that I promptly fell asleep, only to wake up the next morning at 6:00 a.m. I had left the hospital the previous evening. Certain that some disaster must have taken place in the ward, and my termination orders were on the way, I hurriedly got ready, shaved, and rushed to the hospital. Automatically, I inwardly prayed to Swami: "Swami! Please save me. I was busy talking to Your devotee about You only…"

To my utter amazement, the staff nurse greeted me as I entered the ward by telling me that for the first time in many days, even the night staff rested because there was no emergency, and all the post-operative cases were resting comfortably as well. I went to my room and silently thanked Swami. Tears of gratitude welled up in my eyes because for the first time in a week, God allowed me to sleep soundly for several hours, eat properly and take a refreshing bath. I was returning to my work rejuvenated. I know if I hadn't rested that night, some blood vessel in my brain would have burst from lack of sleep and food.

But miracles never cease. Mr. Paramanand Gokul came to me holding a big stone with three stags projecting out of it. He informed me: "Doctor, this has come out." I told him that was impossible. I asked him to remove his clothes, and I examined his urinary passage—no rupture whatsoever. The X-rays also indicated that the stone had passed. This experience jostled my inner being so intensely that I remained lost in MY LOVE for several hours. To remind me of this wondrous incident, I kept that stone for many years afterward.

Once, my elder brother Santosh *Bhayya's* wife, Indu *Bhabi*, discovered a lump in her breast. Upon showing it to the doctor, she was told that a biopsy should be done to determine whether the tumor was malignant. Everyone in the family became worried and began earnestly praying to Bhagawan. Since I was working at the hospital in Amritsar at that time, they depended on me to get the necessary tests and paperwork completed. Her admission for the biopsy was fixed. The night before she was to be admitted, all of us prayed to Swami for her welfare. When she reached the hospital the next morning, Indu *Bhabi* somehow felt that the lump was gone. The doctors examined her and were themselves amazed at how the tumor had vanished overnight. This incident strengthened my early faith in Swami.

In 1976, my eldest brother Basant *Bhayya* developed multiple slipped discs in his back and was in extreme agony. All treatments failed, and he decided to have surgery for the second time. During this time, I had a dream in which Swami took me to His room. In Mother Parvathi's most loving and compassionate form He told me: "No operation for brother. I will cure him without it. Mr. Sharma will help him." The following day I was informed by my parents that something had happened. We received a telegram in the evening saying, "Operation postponed." *Bhayya's* operation was postponed at the last minute, and he was discharged from the military hospital in Delhi.

After a few days, someone took *Bhayya* to a yogic ashram where he was examined by a panel of orthopedic specialists and yogic experts. But they declined him treatment. Sadly, he walked away with his right thigh muscles already beginning to atrophy. Suddenly, someone tapped him on the shoulders and introduced himself as Mr. P.N. Sharma. He asked my brother if he would be willing to undergo yogic treatment under him. (My brother knew nothing of my dream at the time.) Mr. Sharma explained the potential health risks to him—paralysis and possibly death—but my brother gave his written consent immediately. By Swami's grace, within seven days, the treatment rendered positive results. *Bhayya's* condition improved so greatly that he was recategorized to the physical ranking of class "A-1." No physician can explain how his muscular atrophy was reversed. I profusely wept before loving Sai Ma's photo on our altar. "Gratitude" is too small a word to describe all that I felt. <u>By this time, I was completely "WON" by Baba, who started living in my heart</u>

33

<u>as my bosom friend, guide, guru, and GOD.</u> Although pangs for my beloved Krishna continued, I was able to merge the two forms of God.

Swami's vibhuti may be the most powerful panacea man has ever seen. I have seen a few specific incidents with my own eyes, and there are hundreds more that I have heard from others. My first encounter with the miraculous healing power of Swami's vibhuti took place when my mother developed a skin disorder—an allergy to heat. Her condition became so severe that even normal daily activities like cooking and using hot water aggravated her skin. In spite of the various treatments of many specialists, my mother found no relief. Several months passed. One day, my maternal uncle, a renowned doctor himself, brought Swami's vibhuti to her, recommending that she put some on her skin and eat some as well. He used to tell us many stories of Swami and His miracles, but we never believed him and would scoff at the wondrous tales. My mother thought there would not be any harm in at least trying the vibhuti since nothing else had helped her. Within days, the allergy completely disappeared and never recurred. Since this was the first time I had seen Swami's vibhuti work a miracle, it initiated my faith in Him.

During our first trip to Puttaparthi, on September 18, 1981, Sham's wife Usha experienced severe abdominal pain. I administered medicine to her, but she continued to suffer. The pain became so intense that she could not even go to evening *darshan*. Swami came to Sham and me in line and asked Sham: "Where is wife? In the room? I know she is not well." And, for the first time at close range, I saw Swami materialize vibhuti from His hand. Swami poured it into Sham's hand for Usha. No sooner had we given her the vibhuti than she recovered fully.

As I narrated previously, I had been suffering from hyperacidity and a peptic ulcer. Despite the advice of doctors to undergo surgery for the ulcer, I refused because I was well aware of the post-operative complications that could arise. During our first interview with Swami, I was the only one that did not receive materialized vibhuti on entering, and I felt a little sad. After coming out of the inner interview room, Swami came directly to me and said: "You did not get *prasad.*" I answered: "Yes, Swami." He swirled His hand quite vigorously and produced a huge ball of vibhuti, about the size of a tennis ball. I opened my hands to receive it, but He said: "No, open your mouth." Placing His left hand under my chin, He poured the vibhuti directly into my mouth with His right hand. The vibhuti just melted in my mouth, getting directly absorbed. Then Swami struck my chest and upper abdomen saying: "Go. Both of them will be alright. (pointing to my heart and stomach)." From that day, I have not had any heart, blood pressure, or stomach problems. This is how even doctors get cured by the Divine Physician.

I was sitting in *darshan* line on September 25, 1981 when thoughts of Mr. S. Dharam Singh, one of my patients in Dharangwala, came to my mind. The time was 8:50 a.m. He was a severe diabetic, and our efforts to control the illness were of no avail. He developed diabetic ulcers on his feet which led to gangrene of both legs up to the knee. Before coming to Prasanthi Nilayam, I had already sent him to Medical College, Amritsar to have his legs amputated in order to save his life. While sitting in *darshan* line, I was just thinking that I would find Mr. Dharam Singh on a wheelchair with both legs missing when I returned. Instantaneous prayers for him arose in my heart. As I was praying, Swami proceeded directly to me and asked: "What are you thinking? Thinking about Dharam Singh?" He then materialized vibhuti for Dharam Singh and told me that he would be alright.

Upon returning home, I requested my brother to take me to see Dharam Singh so that I could give him the vibhuti that Swami sent for him. My brother said to me: "Nishi, you will never believe what happened." I thought that perhaps the poor man did not stand the shock of loosing both his legs, and he had succumbed to death quickly. My brother told me to go and see for myself. When we went to the hospital, I found Dharam Singh sitting on his bed, his lower body covered. Upon removing the sheet, I became wonder struck at seeing both the legs intact. At first I thought they were magnificent artificial legs that someone had devised. But they were his original limbs.

A unique miracle took place in Punjab on September 25, 1981 at 8:50 a.m. Exactly at the time that Swami came to me and asked me about Dharam Singh in Prasanthi Nilayam, two doctors came to the doctor in charge at Medical College, Amritsar, and introduced themselves as German physicians. They said that they were doing research on diabetic patients having gangrene of the lower limbs. On learning the details of Dharam Singh's case, they prescribed some treatment to be followed for the next seven to ten days. If the patient did not improve, they would proceed with the amputation. One of the doctors was short with curly hair, the other was a tall, old man with a beard. Dharam Singh's operation was postponed and the new treatment was implemented. The German doctors left and disappeared, never to be seen or heard from again. The results were before my eyes. All ulcers healed, the gangrene disappeared, and the legs became almost normal. I cannot describe the happiness that Dharam Singh expressed. From the description of those two doctors, it seems that they could be none other than Shirdi Sai and Sathya Sai Baba. The Divine Physicians performed a most amazing miracle.

On the train returning home from our first trip to Puttaparthi, we met a gentleman from Delhi. He was secretary of the Arya Samaj unit in Delhi. Arya Samajists do not believe in the theory of *Avatars* or human forms of God. He happened to be a heart patient and a diabetic. When he overheard our experiences with Swami, he became literally infuriated.

He said: "No. No God can ever come in human form." I asked him: "Sir, do you agree that the entire universe is created by the mere wish of God?" He replied: "Yes." I continued: "Do you also believe that all of this creation goes on only by His wish and command? Even a blade of grass does not move without His wish." He again replied in the affirmative. I then questioned: "Sir, do you believe that every breath that you take is only due to His wish?" He answered: "Yes, yes." I said: "Sir, if everything is happening as a result of His wish, then why can't you believe that He can wish to assume a human form and come amongst us?" And this is exactly what Bhagawan Sri Sathya Sai Baba has said: "The *Avatar* comes and behaves like a human being, so that we feel kinship with Him. He suddenly rises to His superhuman heights, so that mankind can also aspire to reach those heights." But the man was not convinced. He continued arguing his case. I thought it better to leave him to his own beliefs than to waste our time and energy in arguments.

After some time, he started feeling uneasy and experiencing a fainting sensation. Although he took his medicines immediately, they did not ease his condition. His face became pale and sallow, he was sweating profusely, and his pulse had become feeble. We tried to make him as comfortable as possible, but his facial expression conveyed the agony that he felt. Suddenly, I took out the vibhuti that Swami had materialized earlier for me and poured some into his mouth and rubbed the rest on his chest as I suspected that he was having a heart attack. Within seconds, the man was back to his normal self—laughing and talking as if nothing had happened. He said that he had been feeling choked and suffocated when something very soothing came to his mouth making his whole body feel fresh and rejuvenated. He felt as if some great person helped him through that period of great difficulty and near death. When everyone told him that I had put Swami's materialized vibhuti into his mouth, he became absolutely dumbfounded and expressed his apologies for having spoken ill of Swami. Right there and then, he accepted Swami as God incarnate and begged for His forgiveness. He asked us to give him some more vibhuti and a photograph of Swami. We obliged him, and he literally bowed to that photo. I hope his change of heart was permanent and lasting.

During our second trip to Puttaparthi in July, 1982, I traveled with several Sai brothers in the train: V.K. Kapoor, our state president at the time, Ranjan Jain, world bhajan convenor, Major R.K. Bhardwaj, Y.P. Sahni, and Ranjan Jain's son Basant—a student of Swami's college. During the journey, Mr. Kapoor and I drew up a plan for Sai activities in the state of Punjab for the next three years. At about 3:30 p.m., Major Bhardwaj came running and asked me to accompany him immediately as someone hit Basant with a big stone on the outskirts of Bhopal. Basant was bleeding profusely. I did not have any first-aid materials with me to control the bleeding. I took Swami's vibhuti packet from Basant's pocket, poured some into the wound, and gave some in his mouth. I then firmly pressed the wound and raised his arm. After about five minutes, my companion, Dr. Gupta, came with a first-aid box, but by then the bleeding had completely stopped, and Basant was much better. Swami reduced the injury and the damage it caused to a minimum. Basant's watch had a sticker of Swami on it. The shrapnel that flew through the window hit Swami's head on that sticker, indicating that Swami had taken the impact of injury. The chain of the watch also broke, saving Basant from a fatal injury. Later I told Basant that the scar on his wrist would always remind him of Baba's Mercy.

When I was living in Patiala, my mother-in-law began to suffer from some gynecological problems. A biopsy was performed, and the histo-pathologist suspected a malignant tumor in her uterus. To prevent any unnecessary panic among the family members, I did not divulge this information. The gynecologist recommended a hysterectomy, but since my mother-in-law was anemic, they had to wait for her hemoglobin concentration to increase. In the meantime, I told her to take Swami's vibhuti. Initially, she agreed and took it daily. After a few weeks, however, she stopped. Swami appeared to her in a dream and asked her why she stopped taking His vibhuti. He directed her to apply some on her forehead and to eat some everyday. She obeyed His orders. I was confident that Swami had cured her, but the doctor wanted to proceed with the hysterectomy. It was performed, and subsequent reports indicated no tumor in her uterus whatsoever.

My father-in-law was a heart patient and was not keeping well. Once, he had severe chest pain, and my in-laws called us, requesting me to bring a cardiologist from Abohar to Fazilka, where they lived. After doing an electrocardiogram, the cardiologist diagnosed that my father-in-law was suffering from acute myocardial infarction. He started an emergency treatment, and my father-in-law's condition stabilized.

After the cardiologist left, my father-in-law's blood pressure suddenly fell to 40 mm Hg (systolic), and the diastolic pressure was unrecordable. Although there were three doctors in the house (Poonam's brother and sister were both doctors), and we administered several sets of injections, nothing helped him. His blood pressure continued to remain very low, and I was sure that, at any moment, he would go into irreversible shock. Poonam's mother is a very noble and God-fearing lady who became very distressed with the situation. The last treatment that I had with me was Swami's vibhuti. I gave some to my sister-in-law to pour in my father-in-law's mouth and to rub on his chest. Skeptically, she accepted it and complied with my request. I was confident that the vibhuti would pull my father-in-law through this crisis, and it did. His blood pressure stayed at 40 mm throughout the night, but he remained conscious and alert. The next morning when the cardiologist came, he became dumbfounded on learning the details of our father's condition. There was no way to medically explain how Papaji survived the night. With Swami's grace, his condition gradually improved, and he ultimately recovered. After this incident, faith in Swami began to grow in my in-laws' family. My brother-in-law even accompanied me to Puttaparthi during two of my trips in later years.

I was working at the Civil Hospital, Abohar when a patient by the name of Sandeep Upaneja was brought to me. With enteric fever, perforation of ulcers, and massive bleeding, he was almost dead. His hemoglobin concentration was only .2 gm %, the lowest that I have ever witnessed in my life. The doctor on emergency duty summoned me and declared the patient dead. I began emergency resuscitation measures, but nothing worked. The mother of the boy was wailing. Suddenly, I pulled out vibhuthi from my pocket and putting it into Sandeep's mouth and on his chest, I started a cardiac massage. Swami actually brought the boy back to life. Later, we administered seventeen units of blood to him. The family, which was well-known to me, changed Sandeep's birthday to that day, November 18, 1988, for that was the day Bhagawan gave him a second life. They all became Swami's devotees after this miracle occurred.

In 1982, when I was living in Patiala, a devotee named Mr. G.K. Chopra related some of his experiences to me. Swami had called his family, including one of his female relatives, who was blind, for an interview. This lady prayed fervently to Swami to restore her eyesight and forgive her for any sins she may have committed in the past. Swami asked her to touch His feet. The lady replied that she could not see them. Again, Swami told her to touch His feet. As she bent down, she could clearly see Baba's Lotus feet. She touched them and wept profusely. After a few moments, she again lost her eyesight. Swami then materialized vibhuti for her and told her to rub some over her eyes three times a day. Swami Himself applied the vibhuti the first time. Mr.

Chopra told me that after about one year, she started regaining her eyesight and later fully recovered. In His infinite mercy, Swami reduced the effect of whatever *karmas* she had to carry out.

During the same interview, Swami said to Mrs. Chopra: "You, *pakoda!* (She is obese.) You are having a very serious problem in your abdomen." She replied: "No, Swami, I've never even had a headache, what to say of abdomen." Swami repeated His sentence and said that He would take care as He touched her abdomen.

About one month later, Mrs. Chopra was admitted in our surgical ward for pain in the abdomen which was diagnosed as a case of acute cholecystitis. She also had diabetes, and as her condition deteriorated, she contacted malaria followed by severe jaundice. To further complicate matters, she developed paralytic ileus and went into intestinal obstruction and liver failure. Her condition was precarious; her appearance a mass of tubes and machines. She was already an obese lady, and with the intestinal obstruction, she became absolutely bloated. As she lay in her semiconscious and then comatose state, the doctors helplessly awaited her imminent death. She began vomiting blood, indicating dire seriousness. All had given up hope. I could not simply stand by and watch her die. I rushed to our evening bhajan as it happened to be a Thursday. There I announced that Mrs. Chopra's life hung in the balance, and I requested my Sai brothers and sisters to jointly pray for Swami's Divine intervention to save that noble lady. In the middle of my plea, I started weeping. I returned to my room and proceeded to cry nearly all night for Mrs. Chopra's welfare.

I could not concentrate during my morning prayers, but could only think of Mrs. Chopra and her family. At exactly 5:55 a.m. that morning, August 21, 1982, I saw Swami coming out of one of the photographs in our shrine. He stood right in front of me, saying: "Thinking and praying so much for Mrs. Chopra—Swami will bless her." And He reentered the picture. Immediately after that, *amritha* started flowing out of the photo. I collected it in a plastic bag and madly rushed to the hospital.

As I was running down the hallway, I met Mr. Chopra coming in the other direction. He was looking completely calm and serene. He told me that exactly at 5:55 a.m., when he and his family were doing *Aarti* to Swami, He appeared before them with His right hand raised in blessing and accepted the entire *Aarti*. I told him what happened to me at 5:55 a.m. and showed him the *amritha*. Stunned at the nature of our experience, we went to Mrs. Chopra's room. She was struggling for every breath. We poured the *amritha* into her mouth. I was praying that even if she succumbed to her afflictions, at least she will have received Swami's *amritha* at the end. We both became extremely emotional and Mr. Chopra started reading the *Geeta* Vahini where Swami talks about *Atma* among other things. I could not stand that scene and returned to my room. I prayed intensely to Swami and His heart melted.

After sometime, there was a big "bang" in Mrs. Chopra's abdomen. It sounded as if a tyre had burst. The staff and doctors rushed to her side and found her comatose. After a few minutes, she opened her eyes, and in a low tone asked her mother to get her a bed pan because she wanted to pass motion. She excreted four motions of blood clots, and pieces of flesh. The doctors became nervous and ordered certain injections to stop the bleeding. Mr. Chopra rushed to the house surgeon on duty who passed the injections on to the staff nurse who forgot to tell the next nurse to administer those injections to Mrs. Chopra. On the evening rounds, Mrs. Chopra's doctor inquired about the bleeding which had stopped on its own, even without the injections.

Mrs. Chopra began improving so dramatically that she was to be discharged from the hospital within one week. We were absolutely convinced that Swami had taken care of her, but the doctors remained skeptical. They decided to perform surgery to remove her gall bladder. They would not listen to our pleading that Swami Himself had cured her. All X-rays indicated that Mrs. Chopra was suffering from acute gall bladder swelling, and she was having attacks of pain in her abdomen. This further increased their derision of Swami. They went ahead with the operation. During surgery, they called me in and showed me about one milliliter of pus that they had found under the right dome of her diaphragm. Everything else, including her gall bladder was absolutely fine. I laughed out loud and asked: "From where did this pus appear?" The doctor had no answer. I said: "Sir, Swami wants you to take the credit—that your surgery cured her." He had no response. I know that in their heart of hearts, they accepted what Bhagawan showed them, but our Beloved Lord will not take credit for any act of mercy.

Often, Swami's physical presence is not even required for Him to perform medical miracles. His assurance and the faith of the *bhaktha* are enough to work wonders. In December, 1992, my eldest brother came to Puttaparthi and informed me that our father was critically ill and was rushed to the hospital. On Christmas day, Swami asked about Father and assured us that He would take care. The next day Swami called us all for an interview and told us, among other things, that our father had been very ill for the past three days, and He had been taking care of him during that time. Today (December 26, 1992), He said, Father was feeling better. Swami instructed me to go to Punjab to wind up my affairs there.

I proceeded to Delhi first to see my father. Upon arrival, my younger brother gave me the news. He said that on December 24th, our father was eating, and suddenly, a big bolus of food entered his windpipe causing the passage to be blocked. As a result his right lung completely collapsed and two-thirds of his left lung also collapsed. Father almost died on the spot. My mother rushed to call my younger brother who was working in his medical clinic downstairs. By the time they reached the hospital, nearly fifteen minutes had elapsed. The doctors had almost given up hope of reviving Father. My mother was fervently praying to Swami to save her husband, and Baba heard her prayers. Father was put on an artificial respirator and after sometime, he started improving. After struggling for three more days, his condition stabilized. He returned home hale and hearty. It all happened just as Swami told us in Prasanthi Nilayam. How can we ever thank Him for His Mercy and Grace?

Swami has been kind enough to show me a few of His miracles with even unborn children. During my final professional year in medical college, I was on maternity duty. A very lovely young lady came in dressed as a bride. I learned that she belonged to a very wealthy family in which a child was about to be born after 25 years. Lying quietly on the table, she watched as I boosted the morale of the mother-to-be. Unfortunately, she developed complications followed by fetal distress and subsequent fetal death despite our best efforts. The only alternative was to perform a craniotomy for removal of the dead fetus. As we were preparing to move her to the operation theater, she called me and asked me what was wrong. I tried, unsuccessfully, to keep the truth from her. The poignant moment brought us close; I referred to her as my sister. She firmly gripped my hand and said: "If you really believe that you are my brother, tell me the truth. I give you the oath of a sister's love. I cannot feel the child moving. Why are you hiding the fact that my baby is dead? I only regret that I will have to undergo all of this again before I can have the bliss of being called, 'Mama.' Really, a woman must pay too high a price for becoming a mother." Two huge tears welled up in her eyes. Even I could not refrain from weeping. I said: "Sister, if anything happens to you or to your baby, I will feel that my revered mother—the Holy

Geeta—is a book of lies. I will tear it up and burn it before I see any harm come to either of you." I cried out to my Krishna to come to the rescue of my sister, just as he has come to the rescue of Draupadi. The All-Merciful Lord listened to my cries. Within moments, she delivered a beautiful baby girl, fully healthy and laughing. Madly, I rushed to my room, fell on my bed, and held the Holy *Geeta* in my hands, kissing it and crying tears of gratitude. The precious baby girl was born on October 6, 1973, and she has grown into a beautiful young lady now. May the Lord bless her always.

Another wondrous event took place when I was in Patiala, in Punjab. Dr. Krishna Kumar, President of the Sirhind *Samithi*, brought his daughter to me to be examined by a gynecologist. The girl claimed to be pregnant, but all of the doctors that examined her could find no fetus in her. Several specialists had checked her as well and found no child in her womb. She was a typical case of pseudocyesis, false pregnancy. We advised her to undergo a minor operation called a Dilatation and Curettage (D&C). However, she refused to listen to anyone. She firmly believed that she would have a son because Swami told her that she would. All of my efforts to dissuade her were futile. Finally, I told her parents to take her home and I would have her examined by a professor of psychiatry after a few days. Three days later, Krishna Kumar came to me carrying a box of sweets with the baffling news that his daughter delivered a normal, healthy baby boy the previous night. I simply could not believe my ears. Swami plays His *leelas* in such incredible ways.

My sister-in-law Sangeeta was expecting her first child, and all arrangements were made to have her deliver the baby in our hospital. Her gynecologist was my classmate and an old family friend of my in-laws. Sangeeta went into labor, and we were expecting the happy news at any moment. But, more than 24 hours passed, and the baby was not born. The doctor told me that she wanted to perform a Cesarean section, and we consented. Both my mother-in-law and Sangeeta's mother-in-law were standing by with frantic looks on their faces. Before she could be moved to the operation theater, I learned that there was fetal distress. We all began praying intensely. I took out a packet of vibhuti and asked my mother-in-law to give some to Sangeeta, and put the rest on her abdomen. She did so, and within seconds, Sangeeta naturally delivered a perfectly fit and healthy baby boy.

I was sitting for *darshan* in Prasanthi Nilayam, when I heard Swami inquiring about Dr. Anil who had gone to Hyderabad for his wife's delivery. In an earlier interview that we had together, Swami asked them if they wanted a girl or a boy. Dr. Anil answered that they wanted a son. Swami told them that his wife was carrying a girl, and if they wanted, He would change the sex of the fetus. Dr. Anil repeated that they wanted a boy, and Swami asked: "You want a son or your wife wants a son?" He said they both wanted a son. Swami then said: "O.K. The child is changed to a boy, and you will get him on December 18th." Exactly as Swami foretold, a healthy baby boy was born to them on December 18, 1991.

"*Anityam asukham lokam iman praapya, bhajaswa maam* — that is the command". Having come into this uneternal, unhappy world, adore Me, in order to save yourself."
How can the body escape disease and death? How can the mind escape agitation and anxiety?

"Sathya Sai"

Chapter 6

Leelas

Swami says His *leelas* or miracles are His "calling cards." They merely prove to us His Omniscience, Omnipresence, and Omnipotence. Although I did not physically meet Swami until 1981 and saw Him in Puttaparthi only intermittently, I have been blessed by Him on literally hundreds of occasions. He has come to my rescue time and again and manifested His presence in innumerable ways.

After our first blissful experience with Bhagawan in Prasanthi Nilayam, we were traveling back to Bangalore in a taxi. We had covered only a few kilometers when, suddenly, the car jumped about one foot into the air, and we heard the shrieking yelp of a dog. We shouted "Sai Ram!" Swami had just given me a ring, and I peered into it for His mercy. He said: "You were destined to die now, but I have transferred your death to that dog." And we found a dog, crushed underneath the car. All of us had heavy hearts for that poor creature who performed a great sacrifice for us. Shedding tears of thankfulness, we proceeded on our journey.

When only 30-40 kilometers remained, our taxi stopped abruptly on the road. The driver discovered a leak in the petrol pipe, and so we had lost all our petrol. There was not a vehicle in sight. The few that passed us refused to stop. Left with no way out, we started praying to Bhagawan. After some time, we noticed a brand new Fiat taxi approaching. It stopped when we motioned that we were in distress. There were two passengers and one driver. He informed us that they were coming from Puttaparthi. We were quite astonished at seeing a brand new taxi since we had been trying for days to get one from Puttaparthi, and finally had to rent an old Ambassador.

Anxious to procure some petrol, we informed that driver of our situation. He promptly pulled out a 10-liter can and filled it with petrol from his taxi for us. He gave it to our driver, saying that the next petrol pump was still about 20 kilometers away. We tried to pay him for the petrol, but he politely refused, saying: "Don't worry. I will collect it at a later date." And he sped away in his taxi, disappearing completely from sight at a distance of only 50 yards. Then, we realized that it was only Swami who came to our rescue.

We continued on towards Bangalore, but our car broke down again after 15 or 20 kilometers. The temporary plug that the driver made had given way, and we were back at square one. Either we had to wait for some help to arrive, or we had to send our driver to Bangalore to bring back another taxi. A passer-by told us that the next petrol pump was about 5 kilometers away. I told Sham to sit at the steering wheel, and the driver and I started pushing the car to reach a shady spot. Sham tried the ignition, and the car started. I told him to drive at maximum speed so that the car would cover at least one more kilometer. Ahead, we saw a railway crossing, and the gatekeeper was closing the gates for a train to pass. Seeing us, he just opened the gate for us to pass through and then closed it again. Our taxi came to a screeching halt at the entrance of the petrol pump. How it traveled that distance of 5 kilometers on an empty fuel tank is Swami's miracle.

To our utter dismay, we learned that no petrol was available there, and we would have to go to the next one about 2 kilometers away. In spite of our pleadings, the owner of the pump would not help us. None of the passers-by helped either. Finally, we decided to send our driver on foot to the next petrol pump to bring back petrol in a can.

Then, we saw a shiny new autorickshaw coming toward us from the opposite direction. The rickshaw driver readily agreed to help us. Asking his two companions to get out of the rickshaw, he took Sham and our driver in his auto. They quickly returned with the petrol. By this time, the railway gate behind us had opened. After we thanked the rickshaw driver profusely, he drove off, vanishing into thin air after crossing the railway gate. Again, Bhagawan came to our rescue!

At last, we reached Bangalore tired, but happy, knowing that Bhagawan had taken care of us at every step. After refreshing ourselves in the hotel, Sham and I went to arrange a taxi to take us to Mysore to see Brindavan Gardens. We were left with very little money and could not get a taxi to take us there in the amount we had to spend. Dejected, we turned back to the hotel. Suddenly, one taxi driver called out to us, asking us where we wanted to go. We told him our story: that it was my birthday and we wanted to celebrate it at Brindavan Gardens. To our amazement, he offered to take us to Mysore and back, and we only had to pay for petrol. This calculation came to much less than we expected. We hurried back to the hotel and packed into the taxi for Mysore.

On the way to Mysore, we stopped at a place called Sri Rangapatnam. It is an orphanage managed by a very old devotee of Swami's named Mr. Halagoppa. Swami gave him two small lockets from which *amritha* constantly flows. We paid our obeisance in that shrine, partook some of the holy *amritha* and proceeded on.

After enjoying our trip to Brindavan Gardens, we returned to Bangalore late in the night. We offered the taxi driver fifty rupees as his fee, but he refused to accept anything and drove away in his taxi. The next day we boarded the Karnataka Express for Punjab, carrying with us the Divine memories of our trip. But the cash shortage was still with us. I think Poonam had less than Rs. 10 in her purse when we boarded the train. Even Sham had only about Rs. 100 with him to cover our food and minimal travel expenses.

The train stopped at Vijayawada station early in the morning, and I saw the Blitz newspaper headline: "Punjab Under Fire." A prominent politician who was very vocal against terrorism, had been shot. We became worried for the welfare of the people of Punjab as it was gripped in the fear of terrorist acts. I rushed to the bookstall to buy the paper leaving us with only Rs. 2.50. In the same bookstall, a magnificent copy of the *Geeta* caught my eye. It contained an explanation of each word with accompanying commentary also. I had always been searching for such a version of the *Geeta*. The shop owner told me that it cost Rs. 50. I asked Poonam if she had any other money with her, and she replied: "Absolutely nothing." The desire to have that book grew so fiercely in me that I was ready to pawn my watch for it. Suddenly, Poonam called me to the train window and said that two crisp, new notes of Rs. 50 each mysteriously appeared in her purse, although she had searched it thoroughly several times for money. I told her: "Darling, this means you can keep Rs. 50 and give Rs. 50 to me." She agreed. I continued: "You won't mind if I spend these fifty rupees in the way I feel like spending them. Will you?" I feared that if I brought one more copy of the *Geeta* home, my wife would be very upset with me. In addition, I had already spent several hundred rupees on books and cassettes in Puttaparthi. She replied with a smile: "You can spend the money any way you please. I won't mind." Just then, the train whistled to signal all aboard. I madly rushed to the bookstall and bought the great treasure I had found. Poonam was the first person to snatch it from my hands. Examining it, she was not upset at all, rather she was pleased with my choice of purchase. I was so overjoyed to have that *Geeta,* that I even forgot to thank Swami. Only later did I realize that He was the One to put the money in her purse. Then I thanked Him again and again for His kindness. That "*Geeta* Makaranda" continues to form a treasure in our experiences with the Almighty Lord.

Having received so much grace from Bhagawan during our trip, both Sham and I began attending *samithi* bhajans and other activities with added enthusiasm. Swami returned in kind, amply showering His blessings. In December, 1981, we held a *sankirtan* in our home, and Swami came, making many of the flowers fall from the pictures on which they had been placed. All day I had been wishing for Shirdi Baba's *darshan*, but of course there was no way I could travel to Shirdi. Shirdi Baba would have to come to me. The bhajans went extremely well. While I was performing *Aarti*, vibhuti appeared on the *Aarti* plate. All of us were surprised and very happy to receive Swami's *prasad* directly from Him. Poonam had gone to the kitchen, and by the time she returned, there was not any vibhuti left for her. Since she did not see the vibhuti herself, she did not believe that it had been manifested at all.

After the bhajans were over, our neighbors, Major and Mrs. Chawla came. They had been out of town, visiting Poona and Bombay, and just returned home. Hearing the bhajans in our home, they hurried over. They presented me with a small statue of Shirdi Baba that they brought from Shirdi especially for me. With tears in my eyes, I thanked them and then thanked the Lord of lords who fulfilled my deep-seated desire for Shirdi Baba's *darshan*. I then narrated the vibhuti manifestation that took place just before they arrived. As I was speaking, the plate again filled with vibhuti, and Major and Mrs. Chawla, as well as Poonam, got Swami's *prasad*—produced especially for them.

When I lived in Patiala, Swami used to visit me often, manifesting Himself in the form of *leelas*. Once, I was narrating Swami's stories to my landlord's younger son who was about seven years old. He asked me about how miracles happen. I explained to him that they take place merely by Swami's wish. Anything could happen anywhere. No sooner did I finish this sentence, than the *dhoop* stick on my altar started burning on its own. Both of us were extremely surprised, and I told the young boy that now he has seen Swami's miracle with his very own eyes. Amazed, he went to call his elder brother to witness the miracle. The older boy came and asked how that stick started burning. We told him that it began on its own. As we were talking, a second stick just lit up to prove Swami's presence to the elder son as well. Another time, there were several devotees in my home when the *jyoti* which was burning at a flame of about a centimeter, just shot up to about 1/2 meter, startling everyone present. Within seconds, it returned to its normal size.

Throughout my stay in Patiala, Swami would visit me. His most frequent "calling card" was the appearance of vibhuti. Things began on a small scale on January 13, 1982. I had attended *Lohri* function in my college and was returning home. I found a few specks of vibhuti here and there around my home. This continued for a few days. On the 18th, I attended a state level meeting of Sai devotees in Ludhiana. A young M.B.B.S. student in my college named Sandeep who is a distant relation of my wife also came with me. The two of us were discussing something as I opened the door of my home. Then I was called by my landlord, Mr. Gulati, to attend on his wife who had an abscess in her right index finger. I advised her to get it incised and drained. Suddenly, Sandeep called me to show me the shower of vibhuti all over my room. I called the Gulatis also to witness Swami's miracle. Vibhuti was even covering my bed. Tears of gratitude and reverence rolled down my face. (Incidentally, Mrs. Gulati, refused to get her finger treated. She just applied Swami's vibhuti, and her abscess was completely cured.)

During these days in Patiala, I would feel very close to Swami while meditating in the morning. Even though I slept very little for days together, I never felt tired. This phenomenon continues till today. Swami infuses **shakthi** that gives enough energy to carry out the days' activities effortlessly. On the morning of January 19th, I was about halfway through *omkar* when I felt something in my left hand. Lo and behold, it was Swami's vibhuti. I applied some to my forehead and ate the rest. When I related this to Sandeep, he just laughed in ridicule. Another time, my landlord and his wife smelled the fragrance of vibhuti, and we noticed vibhuti coming out of the woolen clothes I was wearing.

On the morning of January 20th, I found a few specks of vibhuti on the floor. I called our landlord's son to see the vibhuti. I left for my department and returned home for lunch around 1 p.m. I went back to the hospital at 2 p.m. There I was having tea with some of my colleagues when the topic of Swami came up. Our Assistant Professor, Dr. Ashok Gupta, and others all laughed at my "stories" of the miracles taking place. Suddenly, at 2:40 p.m., Sandeep called me out saying, *"Jija Ji,* please come immediately to my room. I am very scared." He explained that he left his room at 2 p.m. to attend his practical exam, and he returned at 2:25 p.m. to retrieve something. There he found vibhuti all over his room. I knew that Swami would show Sandeep His presence eventually. On hearing the nature of Sandeep's anxiety, Dr. Ashok Gupta also requested to see the vibhuti. I most whole-heartedly invited him to join us.

On the way to his room, Sandeep narrated the entire story. He said that Swami visited him early in the morning, around 4 a.m., and said: "You laugh at my *bhaktha,* Dr. Bhatia. Don't laugh and joke. What he says is correct. He speaks the truth. Today I shall send greyish-red vibhuti (Swami even showed him the exact color) to your room and at the same time, I shall also send vibhuti to Dr. Bhatia's room. Do you know your relation to Dr. Bhatia? Three hundred years ago you both lived in the state of Alabama in the southern part of America. There, he saved your life.

And in the next life, Swami made you real brothers. Now again Swami has put you together. Don't laugh. Believe what Dr. Bhatia says." I persistently asked Sandeep if Swami actually said all this to him, and Sandeep replied in the affirmative. We entered his room and found the said greyish-red vibhuti on the floor, bookshelf, tape recorder, and mirror. Dr. Gupta was slightly impressed but wished further proof. He asked me if there would be vibhuti in my room as well. I told him: "Sir, what Swami says in His dream is His wish only, and it is always the truth." I told him we could all go to my room and see the vibhuti for ourselves. All along the way, I was praying in my heart: *"Prabhal Prem ke Pale Padkar Prabhu ko Niyam Bhadalte Dheka / Aapna Maan Bhale Tal Jaye Bhaktha ka Maan Na Talte Dheka."* It means: *"Caught by the intense devotional love of a devotee, God alters even His own laws. He would rather put His own honor at stake than let a devotee's honor be tarnished."* I was asking the Lord to save my honor in my hour of test. The moment that I unlocked my room, the fragrant smell of vibhuti greeted us. A visible cloud of vibhuti filled the air. Full of gratitude, I silently wept before Swami's photo. Dr. Gupta was definitely amazed.

That night Sandeep asked if he could stay with me because he was frightened by the day's experiences. He woke me up around 2 a.m. to tell me that his left hand was getting very cold. I found his hand smeared with vibhuti. It could only be Bhagawan's doing. I reassured him by telling him to pray and to have faith in Swami.

Swami time and again showed us His presence. Sandeep had an exam in microbiology and found his textbook pages covered with vibhuti. On a calendar of Sri Hanumanji in my room, *tilak* appeared at a number of places. The thumbprint was even visible. Both Sandeep and I went away for two days to Abohar and Fazilka respectively. Upon our return, we found a huge "Om" symbol written in vibhuti on the floor of Sandeep's room. A similar "S" was written on his quilt. I requested a friend of mine to take photographs of all this with his camera. We took some in Sandeep's room and others in my room. Only the photographs of my room got developed properly while those of Sandeep's were all blank. We used the same camera, the same photographer, the same roll of film, the same developing. Baba controls each and every aspect of our lives. Everything happens at His will and command.

On the 15th of February, Sandeep called me to show me the word "SAI" written in turmeric powder on his floor. Dr. Ashok Gupta also came to see the miracle. He pointed out a few worms in the powder and said the powder could not be pure or sacred. He even picked up one worm and killed it. Dr. Gupta doubted the genuineness of the materialization and asked me to get a clarification from Swami. I could only pray to Swami to reveal the truth and the significance of what He manifested before us.

The Lord is ever merciful. On the 17th of February at 3 a.m., Swami gave me the opportunity to understand His *leela* by appearing to me in a dream. After showering His Divine Blessings in the form of *darshan* and bestowing sacred vibhuti, He looked at me and said: "Yes, you want to know who wrote 'SAI' in Sandeep's room? Who is SAI? How can anyone write SAI like that? When Swami is Omnipresent, Omnipotent, and Omniscient, what is hidden from him? I always show my presence anywhere I wish. What? Dr. Gupta doubts! He should not! He is a noble person. Tell him he will also see me soon! Don't doubt. Have faith. And you want to know about those living creatures! What are you all? Just wriggling in the meshes of desires like those worms. You are born in desires, live in desires, and die in desires. Only a very few (like those few worms) leave their desires. Yes, that is also my creation. What cannot be created by Swami? Only inanimate objects? No! He can produce anything. Life is at His command."

"The yellow color signifies Enlightenment. Look at the flame. It is burning yellow. Look at the Sun shining brightly, illuminating everything that comes before it. Your *buddhi*, your *gyan*, your intellect should not be surrounded by desires. The six enemies live within. They are *kama, krodha, mada, moha, lobha,* and *matsarya.* They are slowly and slowly eating the intellect and *buddhi.* Yes, kill them—the way Dr. Gupta killed the worm. Kill all those enemies residing in your own self by means of 'practice', *'naam'*, and *'japa'*. Practice discipline of the body, speech, and mind. Tame the mind. When it goes astray, the mind is the worst enemy. It should be in one's control.

Mine are the genuine miracles, born in My Nature. They work at My Will. Don't worry about them. Go ahead. Swami is always with you. Carry out the work more humbly and more peacefully. What if others talk? You remain silent. Silence is God. You lose something every time you lose your temper. Control your thoughts, speech, and action. Others, too, will see the Sai *Sankalpa.* Only buds ready to blossom will grow into flowers. The rest shall have to wait in silence for their turn. The life shown in SAI was genuine. After all, everything is in SAI. Go! I bless you."

One day, I went to Sandeep's room in the junior boys' hostel and could not find him. I inquired about Sandeep's whereabouts from the other boys. They told me that he had moved to the new hostel a few days ago. I was surprised that Sandeep had not informed me of his plans to move. In his new room at the new hostel, I found Sandeep. He said that he thought I was playing games with him, and I was the one to put all the vibhuti and other manifestations in his room. So he changed rooms without telling me. But Swami proved to Sandeep that the *leelas* were all His doing. Sandeep had moved his bed and some furniture to the new room and went back to his old room to collect his luggage and other things. When he brought these to his new room, he found vibhuti spread all over the room, on his bed and other furniture. I did not even know that he had moved, so there was no way I could have done anything. This episode was ample evidence for Sandeep to believe that I was not the one producing all of these extraordinary phenomena.

Despite the fact that Dr. Ashok Gupta had witnessed so many of Swami's *leelas*, he remained skeptical. Once, he asked me to accompany him to the income tax office for some work. While sitting in the office of Mr. G.K. Chopra, we started talking about Swami. Then, we proceeded to the office of Mr. Chopra's senior officer, and the topic of Swami again opened. I was describing some of the miracles that had taken place when, suddenly, vibhuti appeared on the desk and even started falling to the ground from the surface underneath the table top. All four of us were baffled. Still, Dr. Gupta thought that perhaps I was using some chemicals, that coming in contact with wood, caused the formation of the grey ash.

That same day Dr. Gupta and his wife came to my house, after leaving the department only half an hour before. Their facial expressions conveyed complete bewilderment. I asked them what happened, and they only asked me to accompany them to their home. I asked them what was wrong. They said that vibhuti started flowing from a picture of Mother Lakshmi hanging on the wall in their home. They did not know what to do. I assured them that it was only Swami's showing His grace and blessings, and they had nothing to worry about. I went to their house and saw the vibhuti myself. I had not visited their home previously; in fact, I did not even know where they lived. So the fact that miracles started occurring in their home, without my knowledge, convinced them that Swami was some superhuman power.

We learned that Swami would be visiting Delhi from April 7-9, 1982. I was planning to go there along with other Sai devotees from Patiala. As Dr. Gupta's faith was beginning to develop, he also expressed a desire to come with me. Upon reaching Delhi, we found thousands of people waiting for Swami's holy *darshan*. We sat in the middle enclosure or section to get a glimpse of our Beloved Lord. Someone spotted me, and said that I could go and sit in the first enclosure since I was a state office bearer. Not wanting to leave Dr. Gupta alone and afraid of losing him in the enormous crowd, I decided to remain with him there. Swami came out and, when passing by our section, came directly to me. He blessed my photographs, and gave me *padnamaskar*. Dr. Gupta also got the opportunity to place His head on Swami's feet. Dr. Gupta himself reminded me of the dream I had on February 17th, in which Swami told me that he would see Him soon.

Swami has shown me His Presence not only in my own home, but in other places as well. In Patiala, we generally held bhajans in the S.D. Model School, and there I used to give short, ten minute talks on some spiritual topic after the bhajans. One evening, the bhajan session was particularly moving, and I prayed to Swami to give me His *prasad*. He did not respond; the bhajans ended, and the microphone was passed on to me. I cried out to Bhagawan that if He did not give me *prasad*, I would not speak. Suddenly something very hot and burning hit my right hand. The person sitting next to me saw me close my fist tightly. I began the talk. After it was over, that person asked me what had happened. I told him that I would tell him later. The crowd dispersed and the remaining 15 or 20 of us sat down for meditation. When the meditation period was over, I opened my hand and found a sugar candy in it. I told the devotees gathered that in meditation, Swami told me that He would not only give me *prasad*, but He would distribute it to everyone else as well. Then we noticed small pieces of the same sugar candy all over the floor. Everyone partook of the Divine blessings.

We used to hold bhajans once a week in the *Geeta Mandir* in Patiala. After some very stirring bhajans, I was asked to perform the *Aarti*. The camphor was burning in a small bowl which was put on a plate. I was holding the plate when doing *Aarti*. Suddenly, I saw vibhuti appearing in the plate right before my very eyes. Everyone took that vibhuti as *prasad*. Wherever Swami's glory is sung, there He manifests Himself to bless His devotees. That is exactly what all of us gathered there felt in our hearts.

Swami continually blesses all of His devotees, and I have been fortunate enough to hear of His *leelas* in the homes and hearts of others. The same Mr. Dharam Singh for whom Swami sent vibhuti wanted to have bhajans once in his home to thank the Lord for His love and blessings. Accordingly, one Saturday evening, the Abohar *Samithi* decided to have bhajans there. Normally, after bhajans, no food was served, but Dharam Singh was so insistent and sincere, that the *samithi* permitted him and his wife to serve us all dinner following the bhajans.

During the bhajans, the flowers from the pictures started falling one after the other. The ash that remained after the incense sticks burnt stayed in the form of the sticks without falling. Some were standing upright, others were floating horizontally—parallel to the ground. It was really a sight to see. I wish I had a camera to record that unusual scene.

On Monday morning, Mr. Dharam Singh related another miracle to me. His wife casually asked him how much money had been spent on the bhajan. Mr. Dharam Singh laughed at her innocence and informed her that nearly all the foodstuffs came from his own fields and dairy. The only thing he bought was Rs. 16 worth of sugar from the market. Soon after this conversation, he called his farm laborers to distribute their weekly wages. After doing so, he had forty rupees left which he asked his wife to put in the cupboard along with twenty rupees of one laborer who said he would collect his wages the next day. The next morning when Mr. Dharam Singh asked his wife to take out the money, there was an additional amount of Rs. 16 in brand new one rupee notes. They thought someone must have left that money there. After giving the laborer his money, they again put the forty rupees and the sixteen rupees back in the cupboard for safe keeping. In the afternoon, each of those one rupee notes mysteriously turned into a ten-rupee note. Later, they realized the extent of Swami's miracle. Swami first returned the money spent on the bhajan—sixteen rupees—then He multiplied it ten times. Mr. Dharam Singh then proceeded to show me those sixteen ten-rupee notes.

Another strange experience that he narrated to me demonstrated Swami's presence. One day, he and his family members found smoke coming out of the same wooden cupboard. They became worried that some electrical short circuit must have taken place, and the wooden cupboard had started burning. On opening the cupboard, they found an incense stick burning in front of Swami's photograph. No one had touched the cupboard all morning.

On another occasion, a young man came to S. Dharam Singh's house. He noticed that Mr. Dharam Singh had placed Swami's photo above that of *Guru* Gobind Singh Ji on his wall. He told Dharam Singh to remove the photo of the Hindu *sadhu* since no one was higher or more powerful than *Guru* Gobind Singh Ji. Dharam Singh's son, who was only about 6 or 7 years old told that man: "You don't know. He is Sai Baba, the *Avatar* of Shiva—the same Shiva to whom our Tenth *Guru* prayed and asked for blessings. Please go. We will not remove the photo." The boy reported the matter directly to his father. Some of the Sikh inhabitants of the village did not want S. Dharam Singh to follow any Hindu *guru*. Dharam Singh tried to explain to them that Sai Baba was God Incarnate, but they refused to listen. Only a miracle of Swami convinced them. The incense stick burning before those pictures burned out and assumed the form of the most sacred symbol of the Sikh religion, *"Ek Omkar,"* conveying Swami's message that there is only one God. Everyone who saw that became absolutely astonished. The villagers never bothered Dharam Singh again. I went to his home the next day and found the ash in the form of the symbol still hanging in mid-air. Swami is the ultimate divine principle who came earlier in the forms of the Ten Revered *Gurus* of the Sikhs to show the path of Truth, Righteousness, Love, and Peace to all.

When things that we cannot explain take place, we call them coincidences. But in God's Master Plan, nothing is a coincidence. Everything is meant to happen at its own time. Once, my eldest brother, Basant *Bhayya*, went to Russia for some military training. He took two of my books to read. One of them was Baba Satya Sai, by Ra Ganapati. On the penultimate day of his trip, a Russian gentleman called on him in his hotel room. After asking my brother his name, the gentleman asked him if he was a devotee of Sri Sathya Sai Baba. For a moment, my brother suspected the man to be a KGB agent or some other covert group member, but after remembering Swami and His Message, my brother replied that he was a devotee. Then that gentleman told him that he, his wife, and his mother were all devotees of Swami. Swami would visit them frequently in dreams and guide them. All three of them were teaching English in a school there. Swami appeared to his mother in a dream and told her to tell her son to contact my brother and get a book on Swami from him so that they could learn more about Baba's *leelas*. Swami gave her my brother's name and address. My brother was astonished to find Sai devotees in Russia. He gave the gentleman the book after writing "With Love and Blessings from Swami" on it. That Russian brother literally cried with joy after receiving that first book on Swami, since Sai literature was not available there at the time. He thanked my brother profusely and went off with the book.

The next day, the man returned saying that Swami directed him to collect vibhuti *prasad* from Bhayya. My brother replied that he had never received vibhuti from Swami. Both were at a loss as to what to do. Suddenly, *Bhayya* remembered that I had given him a packet of vibhuti given to us by Swami in one of the interviews and a small amount of materialized vibhuti given to me by Swami on a previous occasion. The Russian was extremely grateful for the gift of Divine love. He informed my brother that there were other families in the area who were Sai devotees also, and they would all gather for bhajans regularly. When my brother narrated this whole incident to me, my reaction was ambivalent. I was happy that Swami had chosen us to send His love to Sai brothers and sisters in Russia, but I was sad because the book that was given had gone out of print. I desperately needed that book because Professor Shyam Sundar, Himachal Pradesh State President, had entrusted me with a job that I could not complete without specific references found only in that book. Prof. Sundar asked me a few times if I had finished the work, and I could not reply in the affirmative because I did not have the book I needed.

During one of my subsequent trips to Prasanthi Nilayam, I was going to the bank to withdraw some money, when I noticed a small shop directly opposite the bank. It sold books and cassettes from the Vivekananda Mission. There I found some interesting books on Vivekananda and Sri Ramakrishna Parmahamsa. There was a set of small booklets entitled "Thus Spake _____." In between those, I found a larger book. When I pulled it out, I saw the title: Baba Satya Sai, by Ra Ganpati, the book for which I had been searching for the last several months! I asked the shopkeeper where he got that book, and he was puzzled. He said that the other day, he received his shipment from the Vivekananda Mission, and this book was not included. In fact, he did not have any other book on Swami in the whole shop. The owner sensed my craze to have that book and charged me one and a half times the actual price, but I did not bother about money. I was so happy just to find that book, and that, too, in such a mysterious manner. It was another *leela* of Swami's to enjoy. Once, someone asked Swami about the "communists", and he replied with great wit and humor: "Communist means come you next." And this particular experience amply demonstrates the truth of our Lord's words spoken almost three decades before.

I think one of the greatest miracles that has happened to me occurred in December, 1981. One night, I had a dream in which I saw Baba sitting on a chair in His room. He was holding a golden notepad and writing with a golden pen. I was sitting on the floor near the Lotus Feet of the Lord. Suddenly, I had a great urge to ask Swami for that most beautiful pen. Swami just looked at me and said: "Greedy fellow." There the dream ended, and I woke up to the **biggest surprise** of my life. That same golden pen was lying on my pillow with ink in the tip, indicating that it had just been used. I still have this grand gift of the Lord and will treasure it always.

> The story of the Lord's *Leela* is all Nectar; it has no other component, no other taste, no other content. Every one can drink his fill, from any part of that Ocean of Nectar. The same sweetness exists everywhere, in every particle. There is nothing inferior to mar the sweetness.
>
> **"Sathya Sai"**

CHAPTER 7

BROTHER SHAM

I have made reference to dearest Sham on several occasions. We have experienced many things together, most importantly our beloved Bhagawan. I met Sham in July, 1981. My friend Vijinder had taken me to the shop of Mr. Hari Chand Danwar; there I found Sham sitting. Someone had advised me to wear a silver ring with a white pearl in it to ward off any evil forces, and I had gone to Sham's jewelry store to purchase the ring. Our eyes locked on sight. My mind became flooded with so many thoughts. It were as if I had known Sham forever, even though we had just met. I returned the next day to pick up the ring, but when I got home the pearl promptly fell out. The following day I went back to the store and spoke rather harshly to Sham, but he remained absolutely calm. I was impressed by his equanimity, and our friendship developed instantly into one that I am sure will remain lifelong.

On my 30th birthday, September 27, 1981, Swami called us for an interview. It was my first trip to Prasanthi Nilayam. In *darshan* line Swami asked me: "What do you want?" I replied: "Baba, I wish to sit at Your Lotus Feet for some time." Suddenly, Swami looked at Sham, who was sitting some distance away from me, and said: "Who is he?" A thought flashed across my mind that Swami, You are our Mother and Father, and we are all Your children. So I answered: "Swami, brother." Bhagawan asked: "Brother?" I replied: "Yes, Swami." Then He called us both for interview. When Swami called us into the inner room for a personal interview, I told Sham to go first with his wife and son. He simultaneously requested me to go first as it was my birthday. Baba came out and said: "Both of you come." He proceeded to reveal something most extraordinary. He said to us: "Do you know who you are? You are the real brothers of last life. Swami has put you together again. Live as brothers from now onwards." And we truly have.

For Sham's 30th birthday, we were again in Prasanthi Nilayam together. Both of us were praying earnestly for Swami to bless him on that day. Early in the morning I greeted Sham by wishing him: "Many Happy Returns of the Day." Sham asked me to request Baba to grant us an interview. I said: "Sham, I will tell our beloved Lord that today is your birthday. Let us leave it to His wish."

Swami came directly to us in the *darshan* line and said: "You both go." These were the very words for which our ears were impatiently waiting for the last several days. In the interview room there were ten ladies and nine men. Swami entered the room, and after thoughtfully switching on the fan and the light, He materialized vibhuti for all the ladies. He asked one lady: "How is your health?" She replied: "Better now, Swami." He continued: "Oh yes, but not very good." He materialized a beautiful locket for her with His portrait on one side and "Om" on the other. Another lady from Italy gave her ring to Swami and said: "Bhagawan, change this." Swami said: "What change?" The ring had a huge turquoise stone on it. Swami blew into it three times, and it changed into a brand new silver ring with a beautiful photograph of Baba blessing with His right hand raised. (The next day she was again called by Swami. By the mere touch of His hand, Swami changed the silver ring to gold.)

Turning to Sham, Swami said: "Birthday today!" and with a swift movement of His hand, he produced a beautiful bracelet which He Himself put on Sham's wrist. "Many Happy Returns of the Day. Live a very happy and long life." Swami took us both into the inner interview room. Most of the details of this interview have already been described.

As the interview came to an end, Swami stood up, and we found an extraordinary radiance and glow on His face. He swiftly turned to Sham who was standing on His left and kissed him. I could not believe that Sham was so fortunate. No sooner did this thought arise in my mind than Swami swirled towards me and kissed me on my left cheek since I was standing to His right. Swami then suddenly became very silent and still, as if lost somewhere in the past. Those were moments of supreme bliss for both of us. We found SAI MA standing between us and telling Her children: "Sham, you on this side (left side), and Naresh, you on this side (right side). Love SAI MA." As we followed the Divine order and hugged Swami, we were transported into a world of complete and utter peace and bliss. I really do not know whether we existed at all for those moments, but as we came back into our mortal, physical frames we found ourselves melted like ice. My left hand was in the midst of those beautiful tresses of Beloved Bhagawan. I was holding the Lord's hair firmly in my grasp. It was as soft as velvet and as smooth as silk. (All during this trip a very deep and inner urge to touch Swami's hair had been growing in me. I described the intensity of this desire to Sham on numerous occasions, and he simply smiled at my madness.) I cannot amply express my joy at Swami's fulfillment of my wish. After that we both wept like small children. Swami placed our heads on His chest, and slowly patting us like a loving mother, He said: "Very good boys. Very noble souls. Very pure hearts. Swami likes you both and loves you both. Swami tells others 'Why fear when I am here' but for you Swami is both NEAR and DEAR." Which devotee would not have wished to remain in Swami's lap for ever and ever? But Bhagawan sets a time for everything, and we, too, had to leave that room. Having totally surrendered to our beloved Lord and taking the memories of those precious moments, we left the room.

Both my life and Sham's were changed forever on the fateful night of May 8th, 1984. At 11:45 p.m., I heard a knock at the door of my office. It was Sham's younger brother Kamlesh who had come to tell me to rush to the emergency room because Sham had met with a serious car accident. I immediately went with him and found Sham lying in the van; his condition was horrifying. Having suffered a spinal injury, he would become a paraplegic, with complete motor and sensory loss below the naval. I struggled to gather my withered emotions and face the scene with courage. First, Sham had to be brought out of danger; then he and his family had to be mentally prepared for the new lifestyle that awaited them. The outpouring of love from our Sai brothers and sisters in Patiala was immense. We can never repay their acts of devotion and kindness. We returned to Abohar on Guru Purnima with Sham in a wheelchair.

Both of our families along with a few other Sai devotees from Patiala decided to go to Prasanthi Nilayam and be at the Divine Lotus Feet of our Lord. Sham, especially, was very keen on seeking Bhagawan's blessings. On August 16, 1984, we departed for Puttaparthi on the Karnataka Express. At the Railway station itself, we heard that the Andhra Pradesh chief minister and his government were about to be overthrown. The following day when we reached Secunderabad, the rumors were confirmed. The state was placed under Governor's rule. A surge of violence erupted all over Andhra. After our train left Secunderabad, it was stopped several times by unruly, stone-throwing mobs. By the time we reached Guntakal station at midnight on August 18th, the train was already about ten hours late. There we were informed that the train would be re-routed to Bangalore, and we had the option of continuing on to Bangalore, or getting down in Guntakal. We decided to proceed to Bangalore. After an extremely tiring journey that lasted 36 hours longer than it should have, we alighted in Bangalore and began the last leg of our journey by taxi.

We had traveled more than 100 kilometers when we were met by Dr. Fanibunda. He was returning from Prasanthi

Nilayam and informed us that there were several mobs blocking the road ahead. He advised us to return to Bangalore and stay there for a few days until things became a bit calmer. But the intensity of our devotion to our Lord was so great that we decided to push ahead. After some time, a truckload of people with stones and bricks in their hands stopped us. We got out of the taxi, hands folded in prayers to Bhagawan to protect us. Two members of the group, surprisingly, agreed to accompany us to Puttaparthi. We met four or five such crowds on the way to Puttaparthi, but Swami took care of us each time. When He willed us to reach His abode, who could stop us? The sight of the gates of Prasanthi Nilayam filled us with joy and gratitude. A swarm of people surrounded us as we entered, curious to know how we reached there under such precarious conditions.

We learned that Swami was giving daily discourses on the *Geeta*. What a fortunate time to arrive! His melodious voice, the Divine *Amritha,* filled us with *ananda.* The days passed, and we intensely prayed to Swami to grant us an interview so that we could ask Him about restoring Sham's legs. Finally, the merciful Lord called us in. Just imagine the condition of my heart. I moved to take that cherished brother of mine to the verandah in his wheelchair. On so many previous occasions, we walked side by side on that very path to the interview room. I felt as if the sky were falling in on me.

Swami gracefully entered and, pointing toward Sham, wittingly said: "No election, no selection. You have become a chairman." And then he pinpointed all the problems that Sham was facing. He told us Sham was destined to die, but Swami intervened and converted it to this injury. (I remember that Bhagawan had blessed Sham's wife Usha on September 27, 1981, saying that her husband would live a long life.) We prayed to Baba to restore Sham's legs. He replied that He would do that on "birthday". We asked, "Which birthday?"

Swami answered: "NEXT BIRTHDAY." When that next birthday will come, I do not know.

Soon after this, Sham and his family came to live permanently in Prasanthi Nilayam. Everyone there knows how much grace and love he has received from Swami. Several times, Swami has told Sham to stand up, to walk. But now both Sham and Usha feel they are much happier as they are. Sham said to me once: "What have I to do with those legs which will take me back from here into that mundane and materialistic world where everything that happens is false?" One must learn **surrender, faith, devotion, and patience from this young couple.**

In one of my interviews, after taking me into the inner room, Swami pulled up my left shirt sleeve and, pointing to the watch I was wearing said: "Borrowed friend's watch?" I replied: "Yes, Swami." He went on: "Don't worry. Swami will change that." Then He discussed some other matters. The next day, December 9, 1991, happened to be Sham's birthday. From the time I awoke, I had been praying to Swami to bless Sham. During morning *darshan,* Swami came directly to me and asked: "Brother's birthday today?" I said: "Yes, Swami." He told me to go for an interview. Confused as to whether He wanted me or Sham to go, I hesitated. Swami clarified: "No, you go." Inside, He again said: "Brother's birthday." He moved His Divine hand and produced a beautiful Citizen golden watch. Swami fastened it around my left wrist. Again, I was perplexed and asked Swami if the watch was meant for me or for Sham. Swami confirmed that it was for me. I felt so happy that on my brother's birthday, Swami was acting so kind toward me. The closeness that I feel with Sham cannot be compared.

● ● ●

Chapter 8

Shakthi

Swami has always given me the strength to undergo the tests that have come to me in life. But, in specific instances, I have literally felt the *shakthi* He has poured into me. I know now that it is this *shakthi* that has made me move, work, live, and love. May He continue granting me this energy and strength throughout my life.

Even Sham has been a recipient of this grace. During the same interview in December, 1983, Swami asked me what I needed from Him. Sitting at His Lotus Feet, I said: "Swami, give me *shakthi* here (lifting my hands) and *bhakthi* here (pointing to my heart)." Swami then took Sham's right index finger and held it between the big toe and second toe of His right foot. And Swami continued conversing with us. As we left the interview room some time later, Sham found his right arm completely swollen and red-hot. This condition persisted for several hours as an indication of the *shakthi* that Swami infused into Sham for all the difficulties and trauma that lay ahead in his life.

Later that day as we were sitting in *darshan* line, Swami materialized holy vibhuti for a young boy named John sitting next to me. John's story will be described in the next chapter. After pouring some vibhuti into the boy's outstretched hand, Swami gave the rest to me. While taking my hand into His own, he gave my hand a hard pinch. Seizing the opportunity, I kissed the Lord's hand while it was in my own. Only later did I realize that Swami was granting my earlier request and allowing His *shakthi* to flow into my hands. Truly, without His will and power, none of us can do anything. We are merely instruments in the Divine plan.

Once, when I was sitting for *darshan*, Swami came and stood directly in front of me, while speaking to a devotee sitting next to me. He was standing so close, that His robe nearly touched my face. I placed my right hand over His left foot and began pressing it. Then Swami put His right foot over my hand and caught my index finger between His big toe and second toe. He pressed it very hard for several minutes, charging me with Divine energy and love.

Recently, I was given a big responsibility to carry out, and I prayed to Bhagawan to grant me the strength and the wisdom to fulfill it. Mercifully, Swami appeared to me in a dream, and asked me to take both of His hands in my mouth. Then, He instructed me to suck them, and I tasted the blissful *amritha* on my tongue. I woke up, and the time was midnight. I remained lost in the bliss of that dream for several hours after that and thanked Bhagawan profusely for the strength He imparted to me.

There are several more instances when I have felt Swami recharging me with His Divine energy. Two episodes are described in detail in upcoming chapters. Actually whenever I have been touched by Swami, I feel an instantaneous flow of *shakthi* from Him to me. So often, both on a physical and a mental plane, Swami has patted me, hugged me, loved me. Each time, He bestows His blessings and grace.

Baba endows person with *Shakthi*, with Energy, with Vigour. Pradaaya means "to Him who gifts." Baba gifts vigour, energy and intelligence. For He is *Shakthi Swarupa* the embodiment of Shakthi.

"Sathya Sai"

Chapter 9

Worldly Attachment

In many of His discourses, Swami tells us not to be attached to materialistic things. The world is *maya;* it is all an illusion, He says. Being attached to people, objects, or desires will only bring us pain. The only thing to which we should be attached is the Lord, for He will never leave us or hurt us in any way. It is easy enough to understand this concept, but it is much more difficult to put it into practice. Often, situations arise in which we feel like helping someone or doing some good. To us, it seems that we are performing some *seva.* But we want to affect the outcome of our actions. This is where our trouble begins. We must discharge our duties to the best of our ability, with a clear conscience, and leave the consequences to God. A straightforward idea, but how easily we get entrapped by the world and attached to the results of our actions.

In Prasanthi Nilayam, Sham and I were returning from lunch one day when we met a most charming and handsome boy of about twelve years; he appealed to us instantly. He told us that his name was John, and he was from Greece. We asked him where he was going in the hot afternoon sun, and he replied that he was going for a walk. "All alone?" I asked. "Yes." he replied, confidently. We offered to show him some of the sights in Puttaparthi, starting with Kalpavriksha, the Wish-Fulfilling Tree. As we walked along, John told us that he was suffering from Hodgkin's disease, a deadly cancer. He had already been spleenectomized in the U.S.A. and had undergone both radiotherapy and chemotherapy. Now he was taking cortisone and penicillin while awaiting the inevitable.

The very evening he arrived, Swami called John and his mother for an interview. John said that Swami only talked about his illness, but John wanted to ask him so much more. After all, he was not only a patient, but a human being as well. John wanted to know about life: What is good? What is bad? What should I do to become good? Why do people act badly and take advantage of good people? Both Sham and I were duly impressed with the questions and spiritual insight displayed by the boy. Prayers for him sprung from our heart instantly.

That evening we were sitting in the first row for *darshan*. As Swami came toward us, both Sham and I had silent tears for John streaming down our cheeks. When Swami stood before us, I humbly stood up and prayed: "Baba, please cure this child. He is suffering from an advanced stage of Hodgkin's." Swami said: "Yes, I know. He has cancer." I said to Swami: "Yes, cancer of the lymph nodes. His spleen has already been removed. Please, Bhagawan, bless him." Baba assertively replied: "No recommendation." I continued: "No, Bhagawan, it is not a recommendation, but the true prayer of one of your *bhakthas*." Baba asked the child: "How are you now?" I answered: "Swami, he had fever today. It is not a good sign." Swami did not reply; He allowed me to do *padnamaskar* and then moved on.

All night, Sham and I prayed intensely for John. By morning, our pillows were soaked with tears. There must have been some relationship with him in a previous lifetime for us to be so moved by him so quickly. The next day, we were again in the first row for *darshan*. John was not with us this time. The Almighty God walked directly toward us and said: "You are both praying for him." Suddenly, both Sham and I stood up, and I said: "Baba, please take my life, but save this boy." Sham said: "Transfer this trouble to me." And Swami said: "How can I give it to you?" I prayed: "Swami, my faith says that You are God. You can do anything." In my heart, I prayed to Swami—*Let my faith in You break today or let Your grace flow on this boy.* Bhagawan answered me:

"Yes, I know I can do anything, but everyone must bear the fruits of his or her past *karmas*." As we pleaded with folded hands to Bhagawan, He spoke: "I know he is very serious. This body is just like a water bubble. It comes and goes, comes and goes, comes and goes." At this point Sham offered his only son's life in place of John's. Swami asked: "You want son or Swami?" We instantly replied: "Swami!" He then blessed the notebook in which I was writing this chapter of my autobiography. When we returned to the room, John eagerly asked us if Swami had said anything about him. We reassured him that Swami will surely make him well.

After another full night of prayers for the boy, we sat again for *darshan*. Sitting in the fourth row this time, we patiently awaited the arrival of the Almighty Lord. When Bhagawan came to us, I stood up. He asked me about the pigmentation on John's face. I told Him that it was a side effect of the cortisone. Swami said: "Yes, cortisone effect." I told Swami that John had fever again, and Swami responded with the majestic and familiar wave of His hand. He poured a heap of vibhuti into John's hand.

In the evening, Swami approached us saying: "Matru Naasti, Pitru Naasti..." "No mother, no father, no brother, no relation before birth. All attachments after birth. Why are you so attached to him? Body will go. Don't have so much attachment with a mortal. Have attachment only with Swami. All day and all night you are praying for this child. No attachment with others, only with Swami." Again He repeated: "No mother, no father..." Then, He blessed our photographs. Sham and I requested Swami to write "To John" on one of them. Swami stared at John and said: "Who John? See, don't be so attached to a child." And our Divine *Sadguru* moved on after obliging us by writing "To John. With Love, Baba."

Waves of emotions passed through us. We critically analyzed ourselves and observed that the feelings of love and sympathy had changed into ones of *moha*. We had developed a possessiveness for John which Bhagawan wanted us to remove. Silently, we prayed to Bhagawan to grant us the strength to overcome our attachments.

The next day as we offered more photographs for Swami to sign, He exclaimed: "Daily hysteria! Hysteria! Yes, why do you want Bhagawan to daily give His autographs? You have become crazy." Yes, Swami. We have become crazy for Your Holy Name, for Your Holy *Darshans*, *Sparshans*, and *Sambhashans*. Our hearts beat only for You.

Swami sent word through Mr. Kutumb Rao that John and his mother should return to Greece. We offered our humble prayers to Bhagawan to take care of dear John. We subsequently received a letter from him in Greece in which he mentioned: "My doctors are baffled because my disease has completely vanished." That is the mercy of Our Beloved Lord. Through this experience, I realized that prayers can really move God to shower His Grace on all.

Do not cultivate too much attachment to things of the world, which appeal to carnal desires and sensual thirsts. A moment comes when you have to depart empty handed, leaving all that you have laboriously collected and proudly called your own.

"Sathya Sai"

Chapter 10

SAI MA

Bhagawan Sri Sathya Sai Baba is everything to me. One of His most loving forms, however, is that of MOTHER. He loves His devotee not only as a physical mother, but also as the Divine Mother. On numerous occasions, Swami has loved me in this way, and I will never be able to adequately express the joy and ecstasy that fill me each time. I can only try to jot down the events and details of my life so that people may get a glimpse into the Majesty and Glory of the Divine.

As we stepped onto the verandah after our first Divine interview on September 21, 1981, Swami told Sham and me to wait as He would give us *raksha,* or protection. We sat and waited. Morning bhajans began and ended, with still no sign from Bhagawan. Swami asked for His car and drove away somewhere, waving good-bye to us. The *seva dal* volunteers asked us several times to leave. We persisted saying Swami Himself told us to wait. Finally, left with no recourse, we walked away. In the evening, I was sitting for *darshan* when my younger daughter, Rachita, started crying. I did my best to quiten her, but she did not stop. Swami was already moving on the ladies' side. Since she continued crying and disturbing the devotees around me, I got up to leave the compound. Swami saw me walking away and called me. I turned back. He asked me why the child was weeping. I told Him I did not know. He proceeded to ask me: "What did Swami say in the morning? Swami said 'Wait. Swami will give you *raksha,*' isn't it?" And the Divine hand swirled. He produced a sparkling silver locket with Swami's face on one side and Om written on the other. Swami handed it to me and said: "Put it around neck." I rushed out of the compound in a daze. Swami proceeded directly to Sham and said:

"When you came last, Swami gave you a locket and told you to go back. Then I told you 'I will give you a wife and a son and when you bring them here, Swami will change your locket.' Isn't it?" (Swami told all of this to Sham in 1978 and completed His promise now — three years later.) And Swami materialized a similar silver locket for Sham.

Subsequently, there was a great deal of confusion regarding my locket. People told me that Swami had materialized the locket for my daughter Rachita, who was crying. And Swami simply said: "Put it around neck;" He did not specify around whose neck to place it. I told everyone that if Swami granted me the opportunity, I would clarify it from Him and no one else.

We were not planning to stay in Prasanthi Nilayam that long. Having come all the way from Punjab to southern India, we were supposed to visit several other places in the area. Somehow, I managed to convince my wife that I really wanted to celebrate my birthday in Prasanthi, and after that we could visit the other places. Sham's family also then decided to stay. It was only Swami's grace that we were allowed to remain in Prasanthi. Our accommodations were extended when Swami Himself said we could stay for two more days (to include my birthday).

On the morning of September 26, 1981, Swami came to me in *darshan* line and asked: "Birthday tomorrow?" I was extremely surprised because I never told Swami that my birthday was approaching. I answered Him: "Yes, Swami." He then said: "I will give you *namaskar*." Since it was my first trip to Puttaparthi, I did not know to what He was referring. A devotee told me that I was very fortunate for Swami would personally call me and allow me to place my head on His Lotus Feet. This *padnamaskar* would have a great deal of spiritual value since it was being given with Swami's consent.

During morning bhajans, I was sitting right behind the bhajan singers in the *mandir*. From His chair, Swami was looking directly at me. So much love was pouring out of Swami and into me, that the floodgates were open, and tears ran like rivers down my face. In my heart, I was calling to Bhagawan: "Tomorrow, I am leaving. From where will I get this love, the love that is more than that of hundreds of mothers combined? My Divine Mother, I cannot contain the love that You are showering on me anymore." To keep myself from crying out and disturbing the bhajans, I put my handkerchief in my mouth and bent my head down. Seeing my plight, Swami took mercy on His humble devotee. He stopped the bhajans, had the *Aarti* performed, and left the bhajan hall. Everyone was wondering why Swami left so abruptly, and I felt very bad that I caused all this.

That evening, Swami again asked me in *darshan* line: "Birthday tomorrow? Come." Then I received the greatest birthday gift: the sacred *padnamaskar*. For many minutes I continued, washing His feet with my tears. As I got up, Swami asked: "Happy? Very happy. Contented." I had no words to express my joy.

The next morning, Swami came directly to me and asked: "Birthday today?" I said: "Yes, Swami." He questioned: "Your birthday, or child's birthday?" (Rachita was sitting in my lap.) I answered: "My birthday." He chided me: "What kind of father are you? Your yearly birthday, child's monthly birthday." He reminded me that Rachita was seven months old exactly on that day. Then He called us in.

Upon entering the interview room, Swami asked me: "Doctor, that day I gave you a locket. Are you wearing it or is the child wearing it?" I answered: "Swami, I am wearing it." He said: "Yes, that was for you. Swami gives another for the child." And with a majestic sweep, He made another locket for Rachita. Another confusion arose regarding this same locket. Several years later, I gave my locket to Sham's father for some reason. Since he was holding Sham's locket as well, he mixed up the two and was unable to distinguish which locket belonged to whom. As I looked at the two lockets, I noticed a very small letter 'N' on the side of one. As my first name is Naresh, I took that locket to be mine. In most subtle and discreet ways, Swami clears all doubts that we have. He knows the needs of each and every person, and will satisfy those at exactly the right time.

In the inner interview room, Swami verified: "Doctor, birthday today." I said: "Yes, Swami." He again said: "Birthday today." I answered: "Yes, Swami." For the third time, he repeated the same phrase, and I answered the same. I started getting the feeling that something very important was about to take place. *What followed was so earth-shattering that it propelled me to write this book.* Swami looked deep into my eyes and emphatically exclaimed: "Doctor, 30TH BIRTHDAY TODAY, 30TH BIRTHDAY TODAY, 30TH BIRTHDAY TODAY." Suddenly, I was transported thirteen years into the past when, in Kurukshetra, that *sadhu* made the momentous prophecy: "God has already taken birth in South India, and you will be **FACE TO FACE WITH HIM ON YOUR 30TH BIRTHDAY.**" The magnitude of that statement sent my mind reeling. I could not stem the emotional tide that arose in me. Placing my head on those Divine Lotus Feet, I again washed them with my tears. Like a most loving mother, Swami patted me. I prayed to Bhagawan to always, always, always keep me at His Lotus Feet.

Then, Swami asked me: "What do you want? Ask anything. **I can turn sky into earth and earth into sky.**" This thunderous declaration sounded as if it emanated from the very heavens. I replied: "Swami, only *bhakthi*." Swami replied: "Yes, you have *bhakthi* in you; *bhakthi* is not a toy that Swami can purchase from a shop and give you. It is not a gift that a friend can give to another friend. You have it in your heart; develop it further." Swami placed His hand on my heart and blessed me. With a wave of His hand, He produced a magnificent gold ring with a green stone in it. "This is your birthday present." He asked for my hand, and I held out my left hand. "No," He said, "other hand." (I always had a deep-seated desire to wear Swami's locket and a ring with Swami's photograph. So, I purchased a silver ring from the market outside Prasanthi Nilayam for forty rupees and wore it on the ring finger of my right hand. However, it was fitting so tightly, that I could not remove it.)

Now, as Swami asked for my right hand, I hesitantly pulled it out. Seeing that ring, He said: "Why are you wearing an artificial ring—purchased from the market for forty rupees?" At the Divine touch, the ring easily slipped off my finger and was replaced by the golden one. Quickly, I pulled my hand away from Swami because the ring was burning hot. I was amazed that Swami could hold it in His hand for even a second. Smilingly, He said: "Yes, it is hot since it has just been manufactured. This is real Swami. Swami will be seeing you 24 hours a day from this ring, and you and Sham both can see Swami in this ring whenever you want. No one else can see me." At that moment, I remembered what Mr. Paramanand Gokul said when I asked him for his locket—that Swami would give me many more things.

When we left the interview room, Swami suddenly pulled me back into the room by my arm. He kept my head on His chest, and I heard the most melodious sounds coming from within Him. Only later did I realize that they were the sounds of Pranava and of Krishna's flute. Baba said to me: "Very good heart, very noble soul, what do you want from Me today? Ask." I was completely saturated with the LOVE He had bestowed on me that day. There was nothing left to ask. Again He said: "Yes. Ask anything today Swami will give it to you." Not even a single worldly or materialistic request came to mind. With folded hands, I prayed: "Baba please always, always, always remain with me and bless me for my profession." Swami placed His hand on my head and blessed, saying: "Yes, 24 hours a day, Swami will be with you; 100% He will be with you. And I bless you for your profession—every patient that you treat will feel relief. Go. People will see Swami through you." Finally, I left Sai Ma's lap, drenched in Her maternal love.

On May 31, 1982, I had gone to Chandigarh to visit my sister on her wedding anniversary. After dropping my sister-in-law at her uncle's home, I was coming back on scooter. As I drove around a circular island, I found a bus coming directly at me in the opposite direction. It was moving so fast, that I had no time to swerve. Instinctively, I uttered "Sai Ram" and jumped off to my left since the bus would try and pass me on the right. My right hand was still on the scooter handle. I heard a big bang, and the next thing I knew I was thrown to the ground. Amazingly enough, I did not even suffer a scratch. The scooter was also completely intact. Completely dazed, I drove to my sister's home. She was upset with me because I was very late, and I did not even tell her about the accident since everything was fine. I went to wash my hands and found the stone of the ring that Swami gave me missing. Deeply perturbed, I told my mother the whole story, and she said that I must have committed some very terrible sin for Swami to take the stone away.

For almost a month, I continued wearing the ring without the stone in it and requested Sham, since he was a jeweler, to replace it. He said that the ring was materialized by Swami, and we humans should not try and tamper with it. During our July 8, 1982 interview with Swami, He explained everything. The first thing He said was: "Last year, you came. I gave a locket to your daughter another to you, and I gave you a ring. The stone of the ring has come back to me. How was the accident in Chandigarh? Hadn't I intervened, you would have been crushed under the bus." I requested Swami:

"Please give me back the stone, Swami." He replied: "I'll give. I'll give, in your home." And then He turned to other matters. So many times the Lord has saved me from death. I will be eternally grateful to Him.

Months passed, and I still wore the ring without the stone. Although I asked Sham repeatedly to replace the stone, he refused. Then, one day, Swami appeared in my dream and told me to take the ring to Sham to fit a new stone in it. Knowing that Sham would probably not believe that Swami directed me thus in a dream, I told this to our Abohar *Samithi* Chairman, Choudhury P.S. Bhamboo. Choudhury Bhamboo told me that Swami gave him a dream also in which He told him to tell me to take the ring to Sham. For further confirmation, Swami told the same thing to Sham himself in a dream. We tried many stones in the ring, but none would fit. Finally, Sham tried a dark green stone, and upon both of us saying "Sai Ram," the stone fit in perfectly. In a subsequent trip, Swami approved of the stone, blessing it and telling me that it was alright. His Grace continues to flow from this ring.

In August, 1983, I had come to Prasanthi Nilayam for the Bal-Vikas Training course. After the valedictory function, we were all invited to be Swami's guests for lunch. He personally supervised all the arrangements and joined us in the canteen. What an amazing scene—to be eating lunch with the Lord Himself. My seat happened to be directly opposite Swami's table. He quickly finished His meals and, with His students, started serving us. I have never eaten, and probably will never eat, such a sumptuous meal. Dessert after dessert was being served, and I could not decide what to eat and what not to eat. Even the gods must not have seen such a feast. Bhagawan came to me and gave me some sweets. I became so nervous, that the sweet fell from my hand. The fact that Swami would become angry with me for dropping food made me even more nervous. On the contrary, Swami bent down, picked up that sweet, kept it aside and put two more pieces on my tray. Then He took a third piece and put it directly into my mouth. I will never ever forget that day when the Divine hands of Annapurna Ma fed me like a small child.

Once, Swami was distributing chocolates to His students. There was only one chocolate left in His hand after all the students received the sweets. He wandered this way and that way as if He were searching for a suitable person to receive His grace. For many minutes, every heart was hoping that he would be the lucky recipient. Swami only knows whom He is going to bless. Giving me the most enchanting smile, He tossed the chocolate to me. It carried all His love in concentrated form. As I held it in my hand, I felt as if the Divine mother knew which child of Hers needed the most love at that time. She is always ready to give, give, and only give.

In one of our recent interviews, Swami signed a small photograph: "To Naresh. With Love, Baba." Swami wants us to find the subtle meaning behind all his actions. "Naresh" means "king." He wants us, His children, to live up to the moral standards that He has set. For me to live up to my name, I must strive to be virtuous, fair, and charitable, all the characteristics that a good king possesses. Swami instructed me to always keep that photo with me.

On the Holy festival of Ugadi in April 1992, Swami called us to Brindavan in Whitefield. As He was going to the auditorium to give His Divine discourse, Swami told me to accompany Him. Boys from the college were chanting *vedic mantras,* and Swami walked between two rows of them. I was so fortunate to be on the left side of Swami. He inquired as to when I was leaving for Punjab since we had summer holidays. Then, He asked how long we would be away. I told Him we planned to be in Punjab for about twenty days. Most lovingly, He chided me: "Come back soon. Don't go for twenty days; go for fifteen days." Accordingly we made our plans to return to our mother's home after fifteen days gap. Walking beside the Divine was a unique experience that I will never forget. Swami says: "Don't walk in front of me, for I may not follow you. Don't walk behind me, for I may not lead you. Walk beside me, and be my friend."

Recently, when I was sitting in the evening between *darshan* and bhajans, Swami came out toward me. He acted as if He were about to lose His balance, and I just raised myself to a position where I was kneeling on one knee. Swami steadied Himself by placing His hand on my shoulder and gave a very gentle push with His fingers. I felt as if I were going to hit His belly, so as my face reached His robe, I kissed it. Swami turned to my nephew who was sitting nearby and said: "See, how your mama (mother's brother) loves Me." I was trembling at the thought of physically being so close to the Divine.

On one occasion, I asked Swami: "Baba, there are thousands of people that we see all the time and nothing happens to us. But, when we see You, so many emotions, emanate from our hearts that we start weeping. What is the reason?" Swami replied: "You are all my shadows, and I am Love Incarnate. When negative (you) comes in contact with positive (Me), there is an instantaneous flow of current. Light comes in the form of what you feel and manifest (tears)." May this love always flow between us and our Divine Mother.

Sai Baba means "the Divine Mother and Father." The mother aspect of this *Siva-Shakthi* that graciously grants *Thushti* (contentment) joy, wisdom, courage, self-control, beauty and splendour and *Pushti* (Excellence) in speech, health, wealth children, home, residence.

"Sathya Sai"

Chapter 11

The Ultimate Truth

The ultimate truth regarding Swami is that He is GOD. There are no two ways about it. This truth can only be realized through experience. If one believes that I am an honest man, then all the evidence presented in this book can only point to that one conclusion. From my childhood, I had been attached only to Krishna, and some time was required before I could accept the fact that my Krishna had returned to earth in another form. To reinforce this fact to me, Swami was kind enough to show me His other resplendent forms. There are many forms, but only One God. He possesses all names and all forms.

While reading the Holy *Geeta*, I learned many things. However, whenever I reached the eleventh chapter, doubts would arise in my mind. In this chapter, Lord Krishna shows His Cosmic Form to Arjuna. During our Divine interview on my 30th birthday, September 27, 1981, Swami turned towards me and asked: "Doctor, you have been reading the *Geeta* for the last so many years. What is *Geeta*?" In attempting a reply, I failed miserably. Swami continued: "WHEN I WAS KRISHNA, the first word that Dhritrashtra spoke to Sanjay was 'Dharma'..." Before me, a most incredible vision appeared. It will forever be imprinted on my mind. The form that stood before me was not that of our beloved Swami but that of *Sakshat* Lord Krishna. His face was of the highest *tapasvi*; His eyes were so big that I could hardly see into them. His complexion was as dark as rain clouds, but it had an ethereal glow. A huge, white beard and long, white, curly hair flowed down. The sight was so terrific that I could not stand it for very long. Then He transformed back into our Swami; then again into Krishna and back to Swami. He went on: "...the first word of the *Geeta* is 'Dharma;' the last word is 'Mam.'

So what is the *Geeta?* 'Mam Dharma', my religion. What is your religion?" I answered: "Hindu." He said: "No. What is your religion? Religion means Duty, and Duty is God. I have made the whole of the Universe. I have assigned duty to even a dust particle. If that dust particle is performing its duty, then that is the *Geeta* for it." What a magnificent explanation of the *Geeta!* Although I had acquired and read so many commentaries on the *Geeta*, nothing compared to this. Only the very source of the *Geeta* could explain it in this way.

Swami continued: "Now, see. In the eleventh chapter, Krishna showed Arjuna His cosmic form. You are thinking why could only Arjuna see it? Why others can't see it? Isn't it? Just by saying 'food, food, food,' your hunger does not get appeased. You have to lift the food with your hand and put it into your mouth, chew it, and then gulp it. Only then does the hunger of your stomach get appeased. Now by merely saying 'Krishna, Krishna, Krishna,' you can't see Him. You have to see Krishna as the Divine Principle in even a dust particle. That is the cosmic form of Krishna which everyone can see provided he persistently tries to see that." A great truth, indeed. We will all see and feel Krishna only when we have that urge, that craving, that inner propulsion, and we work on it with intense *bhakthi* and *sadhana* with total surrender to Krishna. One may wonder about this form of Krishna that I have just described as it is not the one commonly depicted in photographs and paintings. But I have described it faithfully—exactly as it was shown to me. Swami showed the same form to Dr. John Hislop, who shared his experience with me. I subsequently received confirmations of this form which I shall narrate.

On July 8, 1982, I asked Swami about personal differences within the Sai organization. Because of such misunderstandings, work often suffers. Swami said: "Doctor, Swami gave nine codes of conduct to the devotees. I know how many are not following even the first step, that is, daily *japa* and meditation. When a person has not taken even the first step, how can he reach the end?" This query stirred me to take a silent vow that I will never miss my morning session of prayers and meditation, come what may. Even if I am traveling in train or bus early in the morning, I sit down and pray.

One day I woke up at 2:10 a.m., and I thought I would sleep for another half hour, as usually I started my prayers after 3 a.m. When I slept, I had a most wonderful dream. I was standing on the pathway that leads from Gopuram Gate to Prasanthi *Mandir*. Swami came out of His room for *darshan*. He was wearing a beautiful garland that reached the middle of His chest. He called me, and I went to bow at the Lotus Feet. I asked: "Swami what is this garland, and of what material is it made?" Swami replied that He would tell me.

Suddenly, He took me up into the air, and both of us started flying. We passed many lands, vast oceans, and mountain ranges without stopping. Finally, we left the Earth also, flying past stars and galaxies. We alighted in a place that was pleasant and cool, with fountains everywhere. Valleys full of flowers emanated an exotic fragrance making me feel as light and fresh as a morning dew drop. Several hundred Divine Beings passed and bowed to Swami. He was still wearing that garland. Then the two of us entered a magnificent palace which was guarded on all sides by many Divine Beings. The inside of the palace was absolutely enchanting, transporting me to a state of joy and bliss.

We continued walking until we reached a vast, milky-white ocean where a multi-hooded serpent was floating. On that serpent was a marvellous reclining couch on which Swami sat. As soon as He sat down, thousands of conches and other musical instruments started playing. Then a most glorious Divine Lady wearing a red sari with gold embroidery came to attend on Swami. She wore many gold ornaments with precious stones on them. I bowed to that Divine Mother, and she raised her hand in blessing. As she smiled, light rays shone forth from her body shedding light on the whole world. She began pressing Swami's feet and before my eyes, Swami transformed into an extraordinarily radiant Divine Being wearing a dark greenish-blue stone around his neck. The garland was still in place. I was wondering what special garland it was when everything stopped and became perfectly still. I felt tranquil and calm and very light. This was the feeling of supreme and utter bliss. I continued in that stage for a very long time. Then Swami came and took me back to Earth.

I woke up, and the time was 5:25 a.m. At the thought of missing my morning session of prayer, I became extremely upset. Jumping out of bed, I hurriedly had a bath and sat down at 5:50 a.m. for prayers. But I could not even force myself to pray because I had broken my vow. The more I looked at Swami's photograph, the more I cried. All I could think of was the enormous sin I had committed.

Then I heard a tinkling of bells and found Swami standing before me in His physical form. He was wearing the same garland that He had been wearing throughout my dream. He blessed me and asked me why I was crying. I told Him it was because I had broken my vow. Then He said: "Tell me why you do these morning meditation and prayers." I replied: "Swami, for reaching You." He asked me: "What do you get from Me?" I answered: "Bhagawan, *ananda*, bliss, peace, joy, and contentment." Swami then asked: "Didn't you get that today?" I said: "Swami, how did I get it when I remained sleeping?" Then Baba asked: "At the time that you normally do your morning prayers and *sadhana*, you were sleeping. What was happening during your sleep?" Then only I remembered my dream: "Bhagawan, I was having Your dream." And Swami questioned: "What did you see in that dream? Where did I take you? What did I show you? All the worlds and heavens, even the Vishnu *Loka* with Lord

Vishnu sitting on the *seshanaag* with Devi Lakshmi, His consort. You were in the *Vaikunta Dham,* enjoying the Highest Bliss, the Supreme Joy for which even the gods yearn. Why should you weep for that time which gave you so much *ananda?* You did not break your vow. It was My wish to bless you with that experience. So, don't worry. I know that when you do your morning prayers you get glimpses of joy in deep meditation. That stage is beyond everything. There is only light, bliss and *ananda.*" I profusely wept and fell at Swami's feet. "Bhagawan, please make my mind feel this *ananda* always—24 hours a day." He replied: "I will do that. Let the time come. Wait. Go on doing your duty." I asked Him: "Baba, what is this garland that you are wearing? I have never seen anything like it before." Swami smiled and said: "Wait, I will tell you." And He vanished, leaving me with a feeling of supreme contentment.

Later that day, I traveled to Abohar from Patiala, where I was living at the time. I was given a magazine called <u>Kalyan</u> published by *Geeta* Press, Gorakhapur. In that particular issue was printed the description that Lord Krishna gave of Himself to Udhava. I was reading the magazine while lying down on the sofa in the drawing room of my home. Shweta had gone to school and Poonam to work. Rachita was sleeping in her cradle, and I was swinging her by pulling the string of the cradle with my big toe. I found the article extremely absorbing. Krishna described every part of His body: from the soles of His feet to the top of His head. I looked up for a second and there was Lord Krishna standing before me. And He appeared in the same form that was shown to me by Swami on September 27, 1981. I thought I was hallucinating. Quickly, I sat up on the sofa, and Lord Krishna, in His most resplendent form sat down next to me on my right. Then Swami appeared and sat on my left. I do not recollect how long I remained in the bliss of superhuman consciousness.

Lord Krishna and Swami were both wearing that greenish-blue colored stone and that garland. I asked Swami: "Lord, you have shown me these two ornaments time and again. What are they?" Baba smiled, and touching the stone, He said: "Kaustubhamani." Referring to the garland, He said: "Vaijayainti mala." These two ornaments will always be found on Lord Vishnu; they are part of His attire. Bhagawan was really so merciful to show me these two glorious things.

In addition to Lord Krishna's *darshan*, Swami has blessed me with the *darshan* of Shiva. One particular Thursday, I had a most peculiar dream of Swami and did not share it with anyone, not even Sham. A few days passed. After *sankirtan* on Sunday, I pulled Sham aside and told him that I wanted to disclose something to him. He said the same thing, and both of us went to my house. Sham told me that he had had a very strange dream of Swami that morning. I told him that I also had a dream of Swami on Thursday. As we started sharing our respective dreams, we realized that we both had exactly the same dream of Swami on two different days. In the dream, we were standing on the same pathway that leads from Gopuram Gate to Prasanthi *Mandir*. Swami appeared and changed into the *Bhairav* form of Lord Shiva. It was a most unusual vision of Shiva in which He was absolutely naked, and his body was smeared with ash. His jattas, or matted hair, were open and flowing; His eyes were burning red. As He looked at us, our wives became frightened and closed their eyes, but Sham and I remained calm, our hands folded in reverence. Our Lord then once again assumed our beloved Swami's form and blessed us. Even as I am writing this, the hairs on my arm stand on end with excitement.

My experience with Swami when we journeyed to the various *lokas* was not the only time that my soul left its physical constrictions. Many times during my meditation in the morning, musical instruments would start playing: shells, conches, bells, flutes. My soul would separate from my body and move upwards. It would roam all over the vast sky, passing over many places. Sometimes, ferocious dogs would chase me, but like a ball, I would bounce high into the air and jump across many buildings. I would alight on some building and then fly again like a bird. As I returned to my room where my body was sitting or lying, I would re-enter it again with severe pain.

I started getting some vague remembrances of past lives. Slowly, the memories became clearer, and my lives during the times of Rama and Krishna appeared vividly before me. During my last life, I was a saint doing great penance when I fell from spiritual heights because of some desires that I could not overcome. My relations in past lives with various people, including Sandeep and Sham, have already been described. Many times, I felt my heart had expanded to such an extent that all of humanity could enter it. My arms were so long that I could embrace the entire creation. Self had expanded into LOVE.

Sometimes, my limbs would grow cold and numb. On several occasions, a white serpent would arise and aim at my head. I passed through experiences of excruciating pain and near death. However, the anchor of Swami and His grace was always present to protect me from everything and guide me through it all.

Another out-of-body experience that I had was again on my 30th birthday. The previous night I could not sleep. At midnight on September 27, 1981, someone entered our room. I got up to see who was there and found Swami standing at the door. He asked me to accompany Him. A little perplexed at the late hour and His mysterious appearance, I followed Him like an obedient child. We reached Prasanthi *Mandir*. Swami took me to the upper room where He lives. I was surprised at the sparsity of His furnishings. There was a reclining couch, a chair, and a few other things. The Kali

Yuga *Avatar* lived so very simply. Bhagawan said to me: "It is your birthday today. What do you want?" I fell at His feet and said: "Baba, only your love and blessings." Swami crossed His feet and tapped three times. The entire Prasanthi *Mandir* was raised about three feet in the air. It was floating, and underneath there was a dazzling array of millions of jewels: precious stones, gems, diamonds, silver, and gold. The treasures of the universe are under Swami's feet. The sight simply dazzled me. The all-merciful Lord asked me to take any amount of that treasure with me. I firmly refused saying: "Baba, I have left the craving for these materialistic objects. I want You and only You." He repeatedly asked me to take something. I kept refusing. Then, Swami embraced me, and I felt like the lost child who had found his mother. A feeling of complete bliss, peace, and joy overcame me. All was calm and serene. This lasted for about half an hour. Swami sent me back to my room; the time was 4:45 a.m. Swami has given me so many experiences with Him, that I can never thank Him enough for all His grace and blessings.

Swami is the Life Force of the universe. Without His will, nothing can move. Once, when traveling from Patiala to Abohar by bus, I picked up the book entitled, <u>Mystery of Jesus,</u> by Janet Bock. In it she describes some very interesting events about the thirteen lost years of Jesus that He spent in India. I came across a few photographs of Swami's materializations. Swami gave Janet Bock a locket with His face embossed on the front. It was very beautiful, and I went on staring at it without blinking for several minutes. A unique visualization occurred. The oval locket became the total cosmos, and in the center I saw a very sharp, black point. It gradually grew clearer and became Swami's enchanting face with His crown of hair. The universe was revolving around Him. Swami smiled bewitchingly and said: "See, I am the center of the entire creation, and everything moves around me." I became lost in His glory and when I finally looked up, the bus had already traveled more than 150 kilometers. Swami showed me that He is the very core of the universe.

The noble souls, the gods, and goddesses living on earth and in the heavens, are all worshipping our Lord. An extremely enlightened man, a *sanyasi* living in Prasanthi Nilayam, once divulged many things to me. This *sanyasi*, who wishes to remain anonymous, came to know about Swami from another *yogi* named Devaria Baba. He told this *sanyasi* that Swami is the *Poorna Avatar*, Lord Shiva and Shakthi come on earth.

The *sanyasi* once developed a boil on his urethra. Many doctors tried to treat him, but he received no relief. He started to worry that it might be some cancer and so, he surrendered to the feet of Baba whom he considers His mother. Swami responds in the role that the devotee calls Him. One night as he was sleeping, Swami came to his room and started massaging him. When He reached the urethra, Swami pressed the boil firmly. The *sanyasi* felt extremely odd, but then felt that it was his own mother nursing him. The next morning when he awoke, his problem had vanished.

Once, when the *sanyasi* was sitting in *darshan* line, a devotee from Kerala sitting next to him narrated a very unusual story. This devotee was sitting on the banks of the Chitravathi River and reading the book, <u>Autobiography of a Yogi</u> by Swami Yogananda Parmahamsa. This devotee from Kerala was contemplating on the *Maha Yogi* as described in that book. Suddenly, he found a young man tapping him on the back. The stranger asked the devotee if he was thinking about *Maha Yogi*. The devotee replied in the affirmative. Then the stranger asked if he would like to see *Maha Yogi*. Upon hearing yes, he said that he was the *Maha Yogi* himself. They both then proceeded to Prasanthi Nilayam for Swami's *darshan*. The stranger *(Maha Yogi)* stood near the Ganesh temple outside the inner compound. The devotee went to sit in the lines. As Swami came out, He moved swiftly in the direction of the stranger and continued looking toward him for some time. After *darshan*, the devotee from Kerala ran to the stranger and asked him what Swami conveyed to him. The *Maha Yogi* said that he had some spiritual problems, and Swami resolved them. There is no need for such elevated people to actually speak with Swami. All communication is mental. He told the devotee that Swami is the very Divine Principle on which all of creation depends. He informed the devotee that many gods and goddesses come to pay their respects to Swami, the God of gods.

One day, the *sanyasi* prayed to Bhagawan to always keep him in the company of higher souls. He traveled to Hardwar and stayed there in an ashram. He was sharing his room with another person who had some unusual habits. The other person never slept but remained awake all night, every night. He requested the *sanyasi* to sleep since he had not yet conquered his sleep. They stayed together for seven days. The *sanyasi* could not stand the spiritual radiations of the other and prayed to him to reveal his identity. His companion told the *sanyasi* that He was none other than Lord Ganesha. The *sanyasi* immediately fell at Ganesha's feet. Lord Ganesha informed the *sanyasi* that he was very fortunate to be living in Prasanthi Nilayam, the very abode of Lord Shiva and Shakthi. This *sanyasi* has spent time with many other gods and goddesses living on earth at this time, and all were worshipping Swami.

I asked the *sanyasi* why so much *adharma* existed in the world where so many noble souls were living. And if all the saints and sages knew that Swami was God, why hadn't they told their respective devotees about Swami? This *sanyasi* told me that the time was not yet ripe for such a revelation. All the saints had been directed by Swami not to reveal that He is the *Avatar* of our age. But soon, everyone will know, and the leaders of the world will be flocking to Puttaparthi to seek Swami's guidance even for state affairs.

Swami has the power to control everything in creation. He is the master of Nature. The first miracle that I witnessed in Prasanthi Nilayam was one such natural phenomenon. We arrived in Puttaparthi on September 12, 1981. The next day, at about 9:15 in the evening, I stepped out of my room only to see a most spectacular sight. Everything was dark, and there were no clouds in the sky. Behind the hills surrounding the ashram, I saw a huge vertical rainbow. Quickly, I called my family and those living in adjacent rooms. We all enjoyed the beautiful rainbow that Swami had created for us.

In 1982, we celebrated Guru Purnima in Prasanthi Nilayam. Early in the morning, I woke up to a most majestic scene. The moon was full, and there was a large halo surrounding it. In the moon, I saw Swami's beloved face smiling down on us. Since I had just gotten up from sleep, I thought I must be dreaming. So, I went to the bathroom, washed my face, took a bath, and returned. But the vision continued. I became so absorbed in that radiant moon that I did not even attend *omkar* or *suprabhatam* that morning; from 3 a.m. to 5 a.m., my gaze was absolutely fixed on the moon. When my family members awoke, I described the lovely *darshan* that Swami gave us from the moon, but they all just laughed at me. They said that I was always lost in Swami's thoughts, and I must have been hallucinating. Rather than argue with them, I kept quiet. When we reached Gopuram Gate, Mr. V.K. Kapoor, our state president, met me with some interesting news. He said that many devotees had Swami's *darshan* early in the morning. I asked him how that was possible. He said they saw Swami in the moon. I told him that I, too, was one of those fortunate ones to see our *Sadguru* first thing in the morning on this holy Guru Purnima day. Many years ago, Swami said that the crowds will grow so large, that He will have to walk across the sky to give *darshan.* Perhaps, this is one of the subtle ways that He will bless us.

The setting shifts to Patiala. On February 20, 1982, I was sitting in our department having tea with my colleagues. The topic of Swami once again arose. One of my colleagues said to me that we, Swami's devotees, claim that Swami can do anything, appear anywhere. If so, Swami should manifest Himself right then and there. I told him that the intense prayers of a *bhaktha* can call Swami anywhere at any time. But if Swami came, would they accept Him as God, I asked. They chided me, saying that first Swami should prove His presence, then they will see. I cried out to Bhagawan to transform the hearts of these atheists, and from the depths of my heart, came this line which I spoke: "He comes like thunder, He falls like a shower, He is none other than Sri Sathya Sai!" As I finished my sentence, the crack of thunder and the flash of lightning were heard and seen. Huge rain clouds over the medical college burst into storm. The downpour lasted for about 20 minutes, but it did not rain anywhere else in Patiala. We were all amazed to witness this play of Sai.

On Swami's 65th birthday, the president of India, Mr. R. Venkatraman was invited as the chief guest. In the evening, we were all seated in the Hill View Stadium for a cultural program. Suddenly, the sky grew very dark, and storm clouds could be seen for miles around. Lightning and thunder began, with fierce rains ensuing. The dignitaries were rushed onto the stage of Shanti Vedika to keep from getting wet. But the thousands of devotees were soaked to the bone, and we were sure the stadium would soon be flooded. Swami walked to the edge of the stage, looked at the sky, and raised His right hand, telling the rain to stop. Within seconds, the clouds parted, and the sky completely cleared. Even the rain god must bow down to the Almighty One.

Not only does Swami have power over the magnificent forces of nature, but He also controls all forms of life, creating and destroying things at will. When I worked at the dispensary in Dharangwala village, I used to pass a military cantonment area. There lived an old family friend named Colonel J.S. Sawhney. I would often drop in at his home and talk about Baba and His *leelas*. One day, as we were talking, Mrs. Sawhney said: "No, it does not seem that Sai Baba can produce even gold from nowhere." I said: "*Bhabi*, not only gold, but He can produce anything that He wants in a mere fraction of a second." She remained skeptical. Suddenly, their orderly, Manayavar, who was also sitting there, intervened. He said: "No, madam. The doctor speaks the truth. I belong to a village near Tirupati Balaji. We do not believe in Sathya Sai Baba, but there is a very poor Brahmin in our village who is an ardent devotee of Sai Baba. His daughter's marriage was about to take place, and 250 grams of gold were promised by him as her dowry. As the wedding date drew nearer, the man became worried because he could not arrange the gold. He did not want the marriage to be called off because the groom was a very good boy. The pressure from the boy's side grew so much that they said they would break the engagement if the gold was not given by a certain date. The girl's father had nowhere to turn but to God. He went to Puttaparthi, and Swami called him for an interview. Inside, Swami told him not to worry. Everything would go smoothly for his daughter's marriage. But there were only two days left, and the man still did not have the gold in hand. He threw himself at Bhagawan's feet, crying earnestly for mercy. Swami just plucked a hair from His head and threw it to the ground. The hair turned into a black cobra, and Swami asked the man to hold the cobra in his hand. The man trembled with fear at the very thought of being in the same room with such a deadly reptile, let alone hold it in his hand. Swami commanded him to do so. Very cautiously, he grabbed the tail of the cobra, and the portion of the tail that was in his hand turned into gold instantly; the rest of the animal vanished. Swami blessed him and said he could proceed now with his daughter's marriage. We were all amazed at hearing this story—that Swami could produce even living creatures at will. When we found those tiny worms in the turmeric powder in Sandeep's room, we wondered about Swami's ability to produce living creatures. He Himself clarified our doubts by saying: "What cannot be created by Swami. Only inanimate objects? No! He can produce anything. Life is at His command."

> 'WILLING' is superfluous for me, for my Grace is ever available to devotees who have steady love and faith. Since I move among them talking and singing, even the intellectuals are unable to grasp My Truth, My Power, Glory or My real task as *AVATAR*. I can solve any problem, however knotty. I am beyond the reach of the most intense inquiry and the most meticulous measurement. Only those who have recognised My Love and experienced that Love can assert that they have glimpsed My reality, for the path of love is the royal road that leads mankind to Me.
>
> I am all forms ascribed to the Almighty: I am the Embodiment of Perfect Peace. I am known by all the Names through which the Almighty is addressed and adored by Man. I am the Embodiment of Goodness; I am Being—Awareness, Bliss, Atma, the one without a Second, Truth, Goodness, Beauty.
>
> **"Sathya Sai"**

Chapter 12

Free Will

Swami runs the entire universe; and yet, He has given man the ability to discriminate and to act accordingly. So who is the doer, God or Man? This point has been argued time and again, often with no decisive conclusion. I have been fortunate enough not only to discuss this issue with my fellow men, but to actually reach a definitive result.

At the tenth All-India Conference held on November 19-21, 1982, I was granted the honor of addressing the audience as a delegate from Punjab. First, I prayed in my heart of hearts to Baba that whatever He wishes should be spoken from my tongue.

"A small pebble from Punjab in the galaxy of these precious gems, rubies, diamonds, pearls, and sapphires, stands before you, my dear brothers and sisters to convey his millions of salutations at your feet." I then posed a few questions to the devotees gathered. My main concern was the implementation of the nine points of the Code of Conduct that Swami has laid out for us. I also asked the officers for suggestions for improving the overall functioning of the *samithi* at local levels.

"To address my brothers and sisters, the delegates of this conference, Baba has given us the word WATCH to remind us to watch our words, actions, thoughts, character, and heart. I request all of you to join me in searching and improving these in ourselves before attempting to improve others. And how many of us are truly following what Swami tells us to practice? The nine steps of Navidha bhakthi explained by Lord Rama to Shabri are now being given to us by Sai Rama as the nine points of the Code of Conduct. We unfortunately follow Swami's teachings in letter only and not in spirit. We call ourselves Swami's devotees, but we are not devoted."

"I would also like to suggest that there be an all-out effort on our part to preserve our *Matru Shakthi*, the force, power, and energy of Mother. I can say with confidence that if Sitas and Draupadis exist with us, there will be no dearth of Ramas and Arjunas or Luvs, Kushas, and Abhimanyus. Regarding ceiling on desires, we are putting ample emphasis on curtailing our physical needs and wants. But what about the wasting of God's most precious gift to us—Time? How much time do we waste on idle gossip and unnecessary things?

"With complete surrender at the Divine Lotus Feet, and with the utmost humility, and devotion, I wish to ask something to Baba Himself. You may call it a small piece of advice from a *bhaktha* to His Lord. Baba, please withdraw this free will which You have given to human beings. It is this that is creating that 17th *kala* in man—EGO itself. Jai Sai Ram. Thank you."

As I returned to my seat, I was embraced by Professor N. Kasturi who said: "Very good. Last part, very good." Many people agreed with what I said; others did not. I did not know how to proceed. After a great deal of soul searching, I heard the voice of my conscience, which I always take to be Bhagawan, saying to me: "Why free will? There is no will at all, whether free or conditioned. Everything is My will."

The 22nd of November, 1982 was a most glorious day; we were fortunate enough to witness the first convocation of the Sri Sathya Sai Institute of Higher Learning. On that day, the newly built administrative building was inaugurated. As Swami proceeded to the function in His Glorious chariot, I was reminded of the majesty of past *avatars*. This must have been how Rama and Krishna traveled on the roads of Ayodhya and Dwaraka. The convocation procession in the evening was simply splendid. Swami, entered dressed immaculately in white, of course. Our *Sadguru* was engaged in uplifting humanity through its vital force—education.

The long-awaited day, our Beloved Lord's birthday, November 23rd, finally dawned. The *jhoola* ceremony that evening was preceded by a massive and unprecedented rush. The Poornachandra Auditorium was absolutely packed. We managed to find a small space right at the foot of the stage. The All-Merciful Lord entered and passed by us. He asked me to do *padnamaskar*, but I refused. I continued praying to Bhagawan to first answer my query regarding free will. Swami lovingly patted me on my back and said the following words that will always echo in my ears: **"Bangaru, Nothing is free will, everything is My will."** I fell at His feet and washed them with the tears of joy and repentance. They gave me solace, courage, and strength to continue.

Subsequently, at the Navaratri discourse in October, 1992 (at which I was present), Swami again mentioned that there is no such thing as free will. Even after so many years, He confirmed what I believed in my heart of hearts.

He is the *Suthradhari*, the holder of the strings that move the puppets and make them act their roles; but He seats Himself among the spectators and pretends He is unaware of the plot or story or cast. The characters cannot deviate a dot from His direction; His will guides and determines every single movement and gesture.

"Sathya Sai"

Chapter 13

Grace

Swami often tells us we do not ask from Him what He has come to give us. Instead of listening to His teachings and trying to implement them in our lives, we ask for petty, worldly things. In all honesty, I have always asked Swami only for His grace, blessings, and love. Even in the one major monetary undertaking of my life, the construction of our house, I only asked Bhagawan for His blessings. Since the completion of the bungalow was only realized by His grace, it was accordingly named, "GRACE".

In 1986, a friend of mine asked me if I were interested in purchasing a plot of land. After an initial hesitation, I agreed. The problem was arranging the necessary money for the registration. As the due date grew nearer and the full amount was not yet collected, I started to worry that I would lose even the advance already given to the concerned party. Our bank balance could not cover the amount, so I had to ask some of our well-wishers to help. Aid poured in from all sources, and we were able to secure a plot in our name. The decision to construct a house of our own was made, and I applied for a loan from the Life Insurance Corporation of India. Ours was the first such application from Abohar, and we had to work very hard to get the various papers and sanctions through the proper channels. At long last, with Swami's grace, the paperwork was completed.

On April 14, 1988, we requested dear Sham to lay the first foundation brick of our home. I put vibhuti into the material to be used for construction, and the work started. I was in dire need of money, and God was too kind to me. Help flowed in from several directions. I could not believe that so many friends and well-wishers came forward of their own volition to help us.

One day, I was required to urgently procure some steel bars for the house, and no money was left with me. Mr. Dharam Pal, my mason, sent a message saying that if the steel rods were not made available immediately, we might have to incur a heavy loss. I almost broke down in my office because the person from whom we had been purchasing material refused to give us credit unless his balance of a few hundred rupees was cleared. Furthermore, the next payment had to be in cash only. That man actually sent a messenger to my office in the hospital to collect the money. I prayed in my heart for my Lord to come to my rescue. Suddenly, the hospital clerk entered my office and placed a bundle of notes on my table and said that it had been sent by the Senior Medical Officer (S.M.O.) to be given to me. When I inquired the purpose for which the money had been sent, the clerk said that he did not know. He had been given a signed, blank check by the S.M.O. with the instructions to go to the bank and withdraw all the money in the account except one hundred rupees, the minimum amount required to maintain the account. I rushed to his home and was surprised when a huge photograph of Swami greeted me at his door. He told me that Swami came and asked him to lend me money immediately. My S.M.O. obeyed the directive without hesitation. Madly, I rushed back to my office and gave the money to the messenger of the shopkeeper. I was overjoyed to learn that the money given to me was just sufficient to cover the needs of the hour. Silently, I thanked my Lord for His instantaneous flow of grace.

Within six months, the construction of our beautiful bungalow was complete. We were filled with gratitude to Bhagawan for allowing us to realize this dream of ours. Everyone seeing that magnificent house felt so joyful. We moved in on November 23, 1988. During construction, the carpenter had visions of Swami on two different occasions. My mason also saw Swami; he said that he always felt as if some outside force was working through him to make him complete the work in such a short time.

When I visited Puttaparthi in November, 1990, I took photographs of our home, "Grace", for Swami to bless. In *darshan* line, Swami came to me and, placing His Divine hand on the photographs, He said: "Yes, I will bless; Yes, I will bless; Yes, I will bless." My joy knew no bounds as it was the Lord Himself who had motivated, drawn, and designed our home. We never dreamed that we could own our own bungalow, and such a magnificent one as that. I prayed to Bhagawan that everything was His alone, and we were only the caretakers.

On the last day of this trip to Prasanthi, a student gave me a photograph of Swami giving me *padnamaskar*. Swami took that photograph and wrote "With Love, Baba" on both the front and the back of the photo. He said: "I bless you from all sides." How blessed I felt. Then Swami asked me what I would do with that photograph, and I told Him I would get it framed. He replied: "Frame Swami in your heart." I said to Him: "Swami, You live in my heart already. No one else can enter there." I also offered Him the photographs of "Grace", and He held them in His hands. Looking at them, He told me: "This is my Mini Prasanthi." The photograph taken in the shrine room of our home has light appearing in the form of flash only on Swami's pictures. When I asked Swami about this, He replied: "This is My Light or Effulgent form." How lucky I felt on that day—having seen and experienced the **ultimate form of Swami.**

Lord of the Universe

Swami along with Dr. A. N. Safaya, Dr. Goldstein and author in the Super Speciality (SSSIHMS) Staff Canteen

Bhagawan along with His Excellency President of India, Dr. S. D. Sharma, Visiting Blood Bank of Sri Sathya Sai Institute of Higher Medical Sciences

Pranaams at the Lotus Feet of Our Beloved Lord.

The Aura of Divinity

CHAPTER 14

SHIRDI SAI AND PREMA SAI

In the relatively short amount of time that I have been in contact with the physical form of Bhagawan Sri Sathya Sai Baba, He has been kind enough to acquaint me with both His previous and future incarnations. One day in November, 1981, I was distributing the salaries of my staff at the dispensary in Dharangwala when I heard someone outside asking for two rupees. After I finished, I went outside to enjoy the warm sunshine. As I sat down, an elderly *sadhu* in red garments approached me asking for two rupees. I reached into my pocket and pulled out two one-rupee coins for him. He blessed me saying: "Always remain happy. Whenever you remember me, I will come. Call me by name and I shall appear before you." He walked away, and I was absorbed in remembering my Lord. I wished to know that *sadhu's* identity and called my peon, Sham Lal to find him and call him back. Sham Lal had been sitting nearby and said he had not seen anyone for the last several minutes. I described the *sadhu* and told Sham Lal that I gave him two coins. However, Sham Lal refused to believe me; he said: "Sir, you must be confused. No one came here." Perhaps I had been hallucinating under the heat of the sun.

That afternoon, Sham Lal and I went to the house of S. Dharam Singh where I used to have lunch. He narrated a strange incident to me. At about 10 a.m., a *sadhu* in red clothes came knocking at his door and asked for food. Mr. Dharam Singh's wife asked the *sadhu* to wait as she was in the process of preparing lunch. He responded by saying that he could even take leftovers from the previous night's dinner: *roti*, onion, and chilly were enough for him. Mrs. Singh searched and found two *rotis* leftover and gave him those along with some pickled onion, chilly, and jaggery. The *sadhu* ate them with pleasure and blessed the couple saying: "Always remain happy. Hereafter, call me, and I will come." When they asked him his name, he said: "Paramanand from *Vaikunta Dham*." Blessing them again, he left. A few minutes later, Mr. Dharam Singh sent his child after the *sadhu* to call him back, but the *sadhu* was nowhere to be found. In fact, no one in the village had seen a *sadhu* all day. The plate in which he ate was still lying uncleaned. After telling them my experience with the same *sadhu* that morning, we all thought it a very unusual coincidence.

I continued thinking about the episode, turning it over in my mind. When I returned home and told my wife about it, she, too, became surprised at the uncanniness of it all. As I lay in my bed that night, the day's scenes were still revolving in front of my eyes. I happened to glance at the photograph of Shirdi Baba hanging on the wall of our bedroom. He was wearing a red robe, and His right hand was raised in blessing. The light emanating from His hand was entering me. Suddenly, everything fell into place in my mind. Startled, I sat up and began weeping profusely. It was Swami who had come in the form of Shirdi Baba to bless us. And He accepted two coins and food from us fortunate souls!

Several years later when I was working at the E.S.I. Dispensary in Abohar, a similar experience took place. Every morning, before beginning the day's work, I would sit down with my staff for about half an hour to discuss problems and take suggestions. One particular morning, a young *sadhu* entered our meeting and asked me to give him some money because he was going to Haridwar and wanted to feed the cows there. I reached into my pocket, and two one-rupee coins came into my hand. Despite the protests of my colleagues, I gave the *sadhu* the coins. My attitude was this: if he spoke the truth, then God bless him, if not, he would reap the fruits of his own lie. The *sadhu* was so happy that he asked me to give him my hand. He put the two coins into my palm and closed my hand into a fist. He then asked me to stand up and open my hand. Lo and behold, the two coins changed into a single two rupee note. Some people were astonished, but most remained skeptical. Then he asked me to put my hands together into the form of a cup. He lifted the sand from the ground and poured it into my hands. As it touched my palms, the sand changed into wheat grains. In my heart, I fervently prayed to Bhagawan and incessantly repeated His name. The *sadhu* blessed me saying that I would never feel the shortage of money (dhan) or food (anna) in my life. Then he said he was too happy with my devotion and asked me to give him more money. I took out my wallet which contained Rs. 3,400 (my entire salary) and gave it to him. My staff members started to panic, thinking that the *sadhu* had hypnotized me into giving him all my money. He took my purse and left.

Everyone started rebuking me for being so foolish. I maintained my composure and said that if my hard-earned salary really belonged to me, it will come back; if it does not, then it was never mine in the first place. Inwardly, I prayed to Swami for giving me the strength to bear it all. No sooner had I finished my prayers, than the *sadhu* came back and returned the full amount to me. He said he was just testing my devotion and loyalty.

Before leaving, he said he wanted to show me one more thing. Raising his wrist to his mouth, he bit a chunk of flesh, about 10 cm x 10 cm in area, causing a huge collection of blood. Then, he asked me for my right thumb to bite. Placing myself at the Lotus Feet of Swami, I offered him my right hand. As he closed his mouth over my thumb, I could feel the warmth of his breath on my skin. I really believed he was going to eat away my thumb making me a permanent invalid. One of my colleagues jumped up to pull my hand away, but before he could reach me, the *sadhu* had imprinted his teeth on my thumb. I felt as if a million volts of current were passing into my body, and I was being totally charged with some supernatural energy. All were watching us anxiously. Throughout, I continued praying to Swami: "My Beloved Lord, I have faith only in Your Lotus Feet. This *sadhu* may be a sage of the highest order, but let my faith and devotion to You remain unaffected." My thumb had become completely numb in his mouth, and I started imagining my plight. What would others think of me? What would become of my family? The *sadhu* opened his mouth, and to everyone's astonishment, including my own, my thumb was perfectly intact and even had a shining glow. I felt as if tons of spiritual energy had been infused to me by him. As if all this was not enough, he then placed his right hand on my forehead saying: "Son, I am extremely pleased with your devotion, and from today I am opening your third eye." A strange light entered that area between my eyebrows. I continued thanking Swami for protecting me from any evil designs of the saint.

As he rose from his seat, the *sadhu* heaped many words of blessing on me. He again asked me to put my hands together. He lifted a little sand from the ground and poured it into my hands. This time the sand changed into a one-rupee note and a ten-rupee note in my very hands. The *sadhu* asked me to always keep those eleven rupees with me. He returned the two coins that I gave him at the beginning of the episode. I asked him to keep those coins with him, and he said that they would forever remind him of my devotion and love. And he left as mysteriously as he had appeared. We were all perplexed by what had taken place.

Still dazed, I returned home that afternoon and showed my wife the notes after telling her what had happened. She, too, was amazed. After lunch, as I lay down for a nap, my eyes rested on Shirdi Baba's photograph. I cried out loud and told my wife that the *sadhu* who visited me that morning was none other than Shirdi Sai. I just did not recognize Him at the time. The Lord Himself was with me for such a long time, and I did not even touch His Feet. I begged forgiveness from Bhagawan for my ignorance and prayed to Him to always continue visiting me thus.

In 1981, I had a most fascinating dream. I was following Swami along a path and then through many fields. There was a railway track nearby. We reached a village, and He took me into one of the houses. There were two rooms; in one, the husband, wife, and son were worshipping the Shiva *Lingam* and praying to Swami. The other room was furnished, but there were no people in it. Swami told me that was the house and the room in which Prema Sai would be born. The name of the village was Gunapalli in Mandya district in Karnataka State. Swami assumed the form of Prema Sai and blessed me. Swami told me that I was the first person on Earth to be shown Prema Sai's form and future home.

The vision was so vivid that I drew this form of Prema Sai on paper much later when I was in Patiala. His face possessed the innocence of a child, and his hair was long and flowing like that of Christ. Subsequently, when I met Dr. John Hislop, and compared the description of Krishna that Swami showed me on September 27, 1981, I also mentioned this dream. Swami had given him a ring in which Prema Sai's face was slowly getting engraved. The image exactly matched the sketch that I had made based on my dream. Many years later, I came across a photo of Prema Sai in a book that again matched my dream. How blessed is this child of the Divine Mother!

Chapter 15

The Mission of Sathya Sai

The greatest period of spiritual awakening and enlightenment occurred when I lived in Patiala. Swami would come to me often, giving me discourses on a wide variety of topics. I used to jot down notes on whatever piece of paper happened to be lying around, and I have compiled them here under the title of Swami's mission. Swami said everything that is written in this chapter; I have recorded it all to the best of my ability.

All religions are basically the same, preaching and teaching the same tenets: *Sathya, Dharma, Shanti, Prema,* and *Ahimsa.* It is we human beings who have created the partitions of jealousy and hatred among ourselves. The walls of envy and the fences of greed that we have erected are closing in our intellect and putting boundaries around the ideals of love and selfless service. We have chained the thoughts of goodness, kindness, helpfulness, obedience, morality, and brotherliness. We have made a mockery of faith and religion. Our progeny have been nurtured with indiscipline and callousness. Forgetting the bright and glorious path of godliness and self-realization, we are treading the dark path of ignorance. Having created a world of disorder, discord, disease, and disturbance, we draw pleasure from sensual objects rather than spiritual pursuits. Our minds have become fixed on matter rather than on the Master.

And what is the state of our Mother Earth? The atmosphere is suffocating; it is being choked by the devils of desires. Yet, we blame God for all our miseries. The Divine Love accepts even this ungrateful act of His children with calm resignation and serenity. That Love, in its purest and most sublime form, can never be enveloped by hate.

The innermost core of every human being has the same basic infrastructure of Divinity. If we can even once reach into that, we will find a fathomless, boundless ocean bubbling with the treasure of *ananda*, the bliss of the Divine Consciousness. Swami has come for this alone: to awaken us, to lead us, to stand by and advise us, to liberate and to lead us to this stage where we can leave the materialistic and mundane world aside and plunge into the inner world of Self-knowledge.

Our society claims wonderful technological advancements in science. What is science? It is "the sum total of all the knowledge when systematically classified, properly arranged, and rightly used." The sum total of all the knowledge can only be known by the omniscient God. We human beings hardly know a finite fraction of the total knowledge, and yet, we boast of the vastness of our knowledge.

There are two types of science: spiritual science and materialistic science. The aim of spiritual science is to reveal the innermost knowledge of the *Atma*. It deals with the ultimate and the subtlest things. It is based on self-analysis and self-experience incorporating self-control. The process involves detachment. It does not require any expensive equipment or laboratories. It gives the most true results, and there is no change in the conclusions drawn. The results are peace of mind, mastery of the Self, and complete contentment.

Materialistic science, on the other hand, is something quite different. Its aim is to reveal the knowledge of nature or *maya*. It deals with the limited or the finite, and the gross. It is based on laboratory knowledge, data, and findings, all extraneous objects. The process involves attachment rather than detachment. It requires extensive experimental equipment for a lengthy period of time. The results are only glimpses of the Absolute truth, and they are always changing. The results are transient physical pleasures and comforts, mastery of matter, and partial contentment.

Swami materialized a beautiful ring for me on my 30th birthday. Initially, I would peer into the ring often to see Swami. He sometimes appeared yellow, white, even orange in the ring. The meaning behind these various colors remained a puzzle. Anyway, gradually I came to realize that I need not seek Swami's physical presence all the time, and I stopped looking into the ring unless, in some dire emergency, Bhagawan's blessings were sought. But, I often wondered about the significance of the shades in which Swami appeared to me and about the lovely green shade of the stone in the ring. Another strange phenomenon pertaining to colors is that many times, when I meditate or even close my eyes, I see two blue lights peering back at me. They appear in a pentagonal shape and flow right into my eyes and forehead.

On February 3, 1982, this mystery of colors was solved. I was living in Patiala at the time, and that evening it was raining outside. Lost in Swami's love, I found Him coming to me and explaining the significance of the following colors. <u>Sky blue</u> signifies spirituality when the grace of Swami is bestowed. <u>Pink</u> is the color that enthrones Divinity. <u>Green</u> denotes heavenly bliss. <u>Yellow</u> is the color of the unique illumination of the intellect. <u>Orange</u> is the color of renunciation, and <u>white</u> is the color that signifies supreme peace and calmness. Then I asked Swami why all these colors were being played for me, and He just disappeared after blessing me.

Now I will narrate some of Swami's answers to my queries regarding spirituality and the state of world affairs. Once, when sitting in the complete and utter silence of my room, I felt as if everyone in the whole world had left me alone. I only craved Swami's love. He appeared before me, and I asked Him: "Baba, when a *sadhaka* feels so aloof and alone that he starts thinking that everyone, including his wife and children, have left him, what should he do?" Swami smiled and said: "The stage when everyone has left you is when

Swami still stands with you. He will never leave His *bhaktha* because He is Apadbaandhwa—the friend who does not leave even in the darkest hours. When such a situation comes, *'Ekla Chalo Re'*, move alone, and the world will follow you."

In one of our interviews, I asked Swami: "Baba, tell me one thing. You have been coming on this Earth for the past so many yugas, as Lord Rama, Krishna, Buddha, Jesus...You have always been teaching man to search God in himself. May I know for what are You searching in this world?" Swami became very serious and said: "I am searching for a true *bhaktha*, but I do not find even a single one to whom I can hand over the reins of the Universe so that I can rest." Suddenly, I said: "Bhagawan, You tell all of us to see SAI in everyone around us. Don't You see Your own Self in us? You will find that we are all You, Swami." Swami frowned at me and then conveyed His blessings in a most loving way. As I left the room, I was trembling. How dare I tell the Lord of Lords what to do? But as a loving mother, Swami just smiled at my innocence.

One afternoon, Swami appeared in my room and I asked him: "Swami, what is the root of all chaos and trouble in the world today?" He replied: "What we think we do not speak, what we speak we do not act, what we act we do not mean, what we actually mean, we never think about that in the first place. What is world? It is called *samsara*, which means coming and going. It is the reflection of your own self. When there is chaos within your own self, how can you find tranquillity outside? Otherwise, everything outside is in perfect harmony. The sun, the moon, the wind, everything follows nature's laws. Only human beings break the laws of nature and suffer. The discontentment and disharmony in one's own self get projected outside as chaos. Set your own Self in order, and you will find everything outside in order."

"Another factor is greed. There is too much on Mother Earth for everyone's need, but too little for even one man's greed. There are two types of people in the world: those who 'have' and those who 'have not'. If those who 'have' can share something with the 'have nots', this world will become so beautiful. Isn't it?" I replied: "Yes, Bhagawan." I continued pondering this point. If the rich and affluent can share some part of their wealth to fulfill the basic needs of so many people, the world would be a much happier place to live.

On another occasion, I was called for an interview by Swami. The Inspector General (I.G.) of Police was a member of the group inside. He asked: "Swami, since You are God, why don't You wipe off the *karmas* of everyone in one stroke?" Swami looked at him and said: "You are the I.G. Police. Suppose you are driving in your official car and suddenly at a crossing you find a red light. What would you do?" The man replied: "Swami, I would stop the car." Swami inquired: "Why? Why should you stop the car? You are in charge of traffic. You can pass without any hesitation, without bothering about what happens." The I.G. said: "But, Swami, it is our law, and if I break it, I may get involved in an accident resulting in anything." The Lord told him: "Yes, sir. *Karma* is also the law made by God, and if I break My own law, there will be chaos and confusion. Therefore, everyone has to reap the fruits of his own *karmas*." What a masterpiece of advice and explanation.

Once, I asked Swami about *moksha*. Everyone wants *moksha*. No matter how subtle is the desire for *moksha*, it is still a desire. Swami answered: "Very good. You should not even keep the desire for *moksha*. You just do your duty, and I will see what is to be given to whom." So, we should be absolutely free of desires to grow in the spiritual realms.

One time when Swami was leaving Prasanthi Nilayam, I asked Him what we should do when He is physically not present. He said that we should recollect all that happens when He is here. I think this is also appropriate for times when we are away from Swami physically.

During one of our interviews, Swami asked a foreign devotee: "What do you want?" She replied: "Swami, I want Your grace." He responded: "You want My grace? For that, you will have to first become three zeros. The first is you must have no relation with anyone; no mother, no father, no brother, no friend. No attachments. If, after that, you still have faith in Me, you must become the second zero: no food, no clothes, no shelter. After losing all that, if you still love Me, then you must be ready for the third zero. People will falsely accuse you and talk about you. If you continue believing in Me, then you will be worthy of receiving My grace. At that stage, I give Myself completely to My devotee."

A small quotation that Swami told me in one of our first interviews has always remained in my mind:

> *"Follow the Master*
> *Face the Devil*
> *Fight till the End*
> *Finish the Game."*

Follow the master, your own conscience; face the devil, all that comes as evil in life; fight till the end, till all bad propensities die; finish the game in that state of illumination of the soul—merger in the Lord.

My mission is just four: *Vedaposhna, Vidwathposhna, Bhaktharakhana* and *Dharmarakshana*. My task is to open your eyes to the glory of the *Vedas* and to convince you that *Vedic* injunctions when put into practice will yield the promised results.

"Sathya Sai"

CHAPTER 16

LIQUID LOVE

After losing the opportunity to earn my M.D., I threw myself into service activities and decided to dedicate my life to voluntary blood donation. And, there was a patient of mine that would change my life forever, giving it new meaning and direction within the realm of blood donation.

One of my patients at the E.S.I. Dispensary, Abohar, was a man by the name of Shafiq Ahmad. A young man working at the local cotton mill, Shafiq suffered from a serious heart problem that needed corrective surgery. Since the surgery could not be performed in Abohar, I referred him to P.G.I. Chandigarh. Because of his low social status, very little was done for him there. Repeatedly, he would come to me to help him, and ultimately I wrote a letter to the director of P.G.I. Chandigarh to take up Shafiq's case as a personal favor to me. The director obliged and Shafiq's surgery date was fixed. However, they asked me to deposit Rs. 26,000 to cover the cost of the heart valve to be replaced. Although E.S.I. was a state insurance plan for the workers of the state, a great deal of red tape had to be cut in order to procure the money. I spent several months visiting authorities in Chandigarh and in Delhi to arrange the necessary sanctions for the full amount. Finally, after about a year, the money was sent to Chandigarh. The reply came that the price of the valve had escalated during this lapse of time, and an additional Rs. 6,000 was needed.

I fervently prayed to Swami to help me. I wrote to the director of P.G.I. Chandigarh requesting him to take the case in the amount provided as procuring another 6,000 rupees would take more time, and the case would be delayed again. The director agreed to schedule the surgery, and Shafiq was admitted. Yet another request came to arrange six to eight units of blood for Shafiq. If blood was not arranged, he would be discharged immediately. Shafiq pleaded with me to help him. I went to the manager of the cotton mill where Shafiq was working to ask him to provide me with a vehicle for taking donors to Chandigarh (a distance of about 300 kilometers.) He flatly refused. Left with no other alternative locally, I approached the Sai organization and the Red Cross in Chandigarh to come to the rescue of my patient. With Swami's grace, the blood was arranged, and even this obstacle was overcome. During this time, Shafiq's faith in Swami grew immensely, and he kept Swami's photo with him at all times.

Unfortunately, Shafiq contacted jaundice in P.G.I. Chandigarh, and his surgery was once again postponed. Dejected, he returned to Abohar and profusely wept at Swami's Lotus Feet in the shrine room of my home. My wife and children had also developed a certain love and attachment to Shafiq. I comforted him and assured him that, with Swami's grace, his surgery would definitely be performed in due course of time. Several times, my family and I prayed to Bhagawan for Shafiq. He began attending our *samithi* bhajans and other *seva* activities on a regular basis.

About six months later, Shafiq tested negative for hepatitis and was readmitted in Chandigarh. Before leaving Abohar, he asked me to be present at the time of his surgery. I promised to be there if no other emergency arose. I gave him some of Swami's materialized vibhuti to apply on his chest and to eat as a token of Swami's love and protection. Due to some official duty, I could not go to Chandigarh for his surgery. However, it was performed successfully. Ten days later, I received the happy news that Shafiq was to be discharged. I planned to bring him back to Abohar personally, but the day before I was to leave, I received a most unexpected phone call. Shafiq's brother informed me that Shafiq had passed away in Chandigarh, and that his body was being transported to Abohar for burial. The shocking news moved all of us to a state of profound sadness. I simply could not believe that that lovable and sincere man, who was like our own son, had left us so suddenly. My family and I were greatly depressed for days. Shafiq's death literally broke my spirit. His last request was that I should be the one to bury him placing Swami's photograph on his chest and vibhuti in his mouth. These very hands that worked so hard for him were the same ones to place him in the earth bidding him a final farewell with the heartfelt prayers that Swami receive him from us.

Subsequently, I learned from Shafiq's brother that the cause of death was excessive bleeding. Shafiq's wound had burst open suddenly, and he bled to death. From that very moment, I vowed that no other patient would ever meet Shafiq's fate. Even if I have to give every drop of my own blood, no patient will die for want of this liquid love. Despite our extreme sadness at losing Shafiq, we struggled to overcome our emotions and accept all that had happened as Swami's will. At times like these, many people try to blame God and lose faith in Him because things do not happen as they want. But Swami has His own subtle way of teaching us many things. Even in his last moments, Shafiq remembered Swami; he wished to leave this world with Swami as his only companion. His faith in Swami never faltered, never broke. If we can remember Shafiq's example, we will have learned what Swami wanted to convey to us. I pray to Bhagawan to keep that beloved soul forever in His lap.

In October 1992, I met a handsome and charming young man named Sanjay Chhiber. He was about 25 years old and suffering from aplastic anemia, a blood disorder. We administered massive blood transfusions to Sanjay, here in Prasanthi Nilayam. When he was critically ill, Swami personally instructed me as to how to treat him each day for about four days. After he recovered from this particular bout with his illness, Sanjay came to talk to me. He asked me to frankly give him my opinion about his condition. I told him that the Divine Physician could cure any illness. We spent many hours completely lost in talking about Swami and sharing the warmth of His love. Before leaving my office, Sanjay told me he knew his days were numbered. He felt that he had completed the work Swami sent him on earth to do, and he was ready if the Lord called. Sanjay wanted Swami to know that he had learned his lessons well; as a bright and obedient student, he had absorbed all that the Divine teacher taught him. I was impressed by his fortitude and acceptance of such a fate. He was not at all bitter or cold, although he had every right to be. Sanjay's loving personality made me feel a deep kinship with him, and I prayed to Swami for his welfare.

In December of that same year, Swami sent Sanjay to the U.S.A., after telling him that He would marry him in February. Sanjay was employed by a well-known pharmaceutical company in America. He thoughtfully took the time to send me a great deal of literature that I requested. I continued sending him my love and praying for him. Suddenly, one day, I was informed that Sanjay passed away undergoing treatment in the U.S.A. The tragic news struck something deep in my soul. I felt particularly bad that such a noble soul was gone at a very young age.

Subsequently, his parents returned, and I met them to offer my condolences. They told me that during Sanjay's last days in the hospital, both they and he saw Swami physically holding Sanjay in His arms. He breathed his last in the Lord's arms, before merging with Him in the marriage that is eternal. Never in my life will I forget what this young man taught me. When death comes, it is not the age that matters, but the actions that one performs. Sanjay was a student who learned the Divine message so well, that he became a teacher for all of us who came in contact with him.

I had decided that I would celebrate all the happy occasions in my life by sharing the gift of liquid love, blood, with someone needy. I donate blood on Bhagawan's birthday, my children's birthday, my marriage anniversary. At Swami's 60th birthday celebrations, I was working at the medical camp next to the Poornachandra Auditorium. Since Swami's birthday was rapidly approaching, I had been wondering if and how I could donate blood in Prasanthi Nilayam.

On November 22, 1985, I was working in our provisional lab with Dr. Subramanium, Professor of Biochemistry at Guntur Medical College. He gave me the slide of a blood film to examine under the microscope. I concluded that the patient had acute leukemia, a blood cancer, and probably had a very low level of hemoglobin. The patient's son happened to be a paramedical working with us, and he told me that his father had been bleeding excessively, confirming the low level of hemoglobin. The patient required a blood transfusion, but the son could not arrange the blood. I asked him if he knew his father's blood group, and he replied: "Yes sir, O positive." Immediately, I requested him to accompany me to the hospital. Both my brother-in-law and I were O positive, and we would donate our blood for the patient. Inwardly, I thanked Swami for the opportunity to be of service and for fulfilling my inner wish to give blood on His birthday.

At the hospital, I explained everything to the medical superintendent, Dr. Chary, an elderly gentleman who had dedicated everything at Swami's Lotus Feet. He agreed to take our blood and transfuse it to the patient. As I lay on the couch donating blood, I saw Swami's photograph on the wall. Both His hands were raised in blessing. Sitting up after the donation was over, I said to Bhagawan in my heart: "Lord, You know that today I have donated blood for the 36th time. Thank you, Swami."

Suddenly, a nurse came rushing in to inform us that Swami was coming to the hospital. We all came and stood at the entrance. Swami's car arrived, and He alighted in front of us. He asked Dr. Chary about the condition of the leukemic patient and the details of the blood transfusion. Dr. Chary told Swami that blood had been arranged and that I had donated blood for the transfusion. Swami came to me, blessed me by patting me on the back and giving me vibhuti. Smilingly, He asked: "How was this blood donation, sir?" My emotions could not be contained, and with tears flowing down my face, I answered: "Swami, I will never forget this blood donation." Swami waved and moved on, leaving behind a trail of blessings and memories that I will always treasure. At that time, I could have never imagined that THAT blood donation would be the figurative foundation stone upon which a large building would be constructed—that Swami had chosen this humble servant for a task to perform in the years to come.

> Love, respect, tolerance, mutual co-operation, forbearance-these must flow from the hearts of all towards all, you are all limbs of one body - the Sai body. Love is joy, Love is power, Love is light, Love is God. If at all you want to label Me, then call Me *Premswarup*. Love is the keynote of harmony; work, worship and wisdom are the three stages on the godward path. Love leads to expansion; hatred leads to contraction. Love lives by giving and forgiving, self lives by getting and forgetting. Selfless love is the source of happiness, truth, peace, sacrifice, endurance, and all other higher values of life.
>
> **"Sathya Sai"**

CHAPTER 17

SRI SATHYA SAI INSTITUTE OF HIGHER MEDICAL SCIENCES

The desire to come and live at Swami's Lotus Feet permanently had been burning within me right from the beginning. Swami is a loving God who fulfills the sincere and true yearnings of His *bhakthas*, but everything unfolds to us only in its proper time. Right on our very first trip to Prasanthi Nilayam in 1981, I expressed a wish to come here for good. Sitting in *darshan* line on September 25, I began to pray to Swami to give me the chance to live and work in Prasanthi as a doctor in His small hospital. As Swami approached our side, my prayers intensified. He looked at me and continued on. Inside I cried out: "Swami, won't you listen to my silent prayers?" Swami retraced His footsteps, walking backwards and stopping in front of me. He questioned: "Aren't they My people? Isn't that My work?" He made me realize that my work in Punjab was no less important than any work being done in Prasanthi. Every patient is His, each work completed is His.

After losing the chance to earn my M.D., I went to Bhagawan to seek His blessings in 1983. After He had consoled me, I prayed to Bhagawan: "Swami, please give me a job here. My wife is a dental surgeon. She may also be asked to come." Swami replied: "Wait. You are ready. Wife is not yet ready." I accepted the Lord's command and waited for the long-awaited day when He would call me to Him.

In November, 1990, I was in Prasanthi Nilayam again for Swami's 65th birthday. I informed Dr. A. Bapiraju that I was a doctor and was willing to render my services if need be. The very next day he informed me that Swami wants all of His students to have a medical examination. What a unique fortune for me—to come in contact with those young buds blossoming in the light of SAI. To carry out this project, I proceeded to Bangalore, and with the help of another doctor there, obtained the necessary materials and forms for the physical examinations. We spent the next five days examining Swami's students. Everyday we received Swami's *prasad*, eating with those innocent children. On November 22, 1990, Swami laid the foundation for the Sri Sathya Sai Institute of Higher Medical Sciences, an unparalleled institution to come. At that moment, I prayed with all my heart and soul to Bhagawan that if I could get any job there, my life would be fulfilled. Later, I met Dr. A.N. Safaya, the future director of the hospital, and I gave him my resume with the humble request and prayers to consider allowing me to come and serve Swami in His most spectacular institution.

The day of celebration finally arrived—Swami's birthday. About 350,000 devotees were present on this momentous occasion to just have a glimpse of their Lord. Swami cut a huge 100 kilogram birthday cake prepared by His students. On that day, I felt I was the luckiest person on Earth because no one else received what I did. I was given the candles in the shape of numbers six and five, along with the decoration material of the cake. They will form a lifelong treasure, and generations to come will see and remember that these candles were lit by God Himself.

In September, 1991, I received a letter from my mother in which she informed me about an advertisement for the various posts of the Sri Sathya Sai Institute of Higher Medical Sciences (SSSIHMS). I sent my application and biodata with Sham's father who was going to Prasanthi Nilayam. To be allowed to work in that hospital was the ultimate dream of my life. I would be permanently at the Lotus Feet of my Lord and serving the needy and poor always. There could be no greater opportunity for me. Bhagawan alone knew the yearning of my heart for this wish.

On October 28, 1991, I received a registered letter carrying the HAPPIEST NEWS of my entire life. All-merciful Swami heard my prayers and blessed me to be one of His humble instruments at the Greatest Medical Institute in the world. He had chosen me to be the Blood Bank Officer at Sri Sathya Sai Institute of Higher Medical Sciences. It was really the chance of a lifetime. In a matter of seconds, I made up my mind to leave everything and join. Friends and well-wishers were stunned at my sudden decision to leave, and many tried to dissuade me. They told me not to leave my comfortable government job with a good salary, position, and benefits. For me, there was only one point to be argued, and it was that NOTHING compares to being in the physical presence of Bhagawan. I was ready to leave everything in the world for that alone.

I proceeded to Delhi to receive some training at the All India Institute of Medical Sciences. My wife and children continued living in Abohar, and we all prayed that Swami would reunite us soon. I reached Prasanthi Nilayam on November 18, 1991, and the next day I went to the Poornachandra Auditorium to meet Bhagawan. Upon seeing me, Swami nearly ran over to me and embraced me heartily. He took my tiny hands in His own and said: "Bhatia, I have selected you for a specific purpose. My blood bank should be the BEST in the world." I replied: "Yes, Bhagawan, it will be with Your grace and blessings." For about 20-25 minutes, Swami held my hands and infused energy into me to carry out the task for which I had been selected. In reality, I am not the one to do anything. It is He who is the Inner Motivator and Doer of everything. We are all His instruments. Swami gave me instructions and advice about my job and blessed me profusely before leaving. Fully charged with Divine blessings and love, I left for the work set out for me.

Since the hospital was to be inaugurated on November 22nd, and cardio-thoracic surgery was to be undertaken, there was not much time left to get everything ready. The magnificence of Swami's plan now unfolds. The previous year I had been present to help in arranging and performing medical checkups of all of Swami's students. At that time, we checked everyone's blood groups. This made it possible to arrange, in a short amount of time, a blood donation camp to collect blood for the first few surgeries to be performed. We fixed the camp—the first of its kind—for Nov. 21, 1991.

I sought Bhagawan's permission to be the first blood donor in the blood bank of His institute. Swami graciously granted me that honor. After receiving His blessings, we proceeded to the Boys' hostel, and collected the required number of blood units. At about 8:30 in the evening, I finally got a chance to go to the blood bank in the newly constructed hospital building. Everything lay helter-skelter. Chaos prevailed, and I could not imagine it functioning as a hospital the next day. From past experience, however, I knew that Swami creates such situations to test our faith in Him. Within a few hours, only a handful of us were able to set up all the instruments and arrange everything so beautifully that we even got a couple of hours of sleep before the long day ahead.

Throughout the night, thousands of *seva dal* members, students, and staff worked to put the finishing touches on the hospital building. It looked more like a Divine temple than a hospital. There are no words to describe the beauty and grandeur of the Institute spreading over about 100 acres of land and covering 350,000 square feet. Every particle conveyed the vibrations of Swami and His grace. The fact that it was constructed in only 5 1/2 months is a miracle in itself.

Our hearts were palpitating with anticipation for Swami to visit the hospital for the inaugural function. He finally arrived with Shri P.V. Narsimha Rao, our Prime Minister, the chief guest. Amidst the chanting of the *vedas* and the sacred names of the Lord, the hospital was formally inaugurated.

Swami took His guests on a tour of the hospital showing them everything that had been established. The Prime Minister and others were totally baffled at the sight of it all. He said that the inauguration of the hospital and the university convocation were mere pretenses for Bhagawan to bring him here and grant His blessings, which were much needed by him and by the country at that time.

As we were very busy in the hospital, we could not attend the festivities associated with Swami's birthday. Silently, from my department, I conveyed my *pranams* to Him. And within hours, He responded by coming to the hospital to bless us. Really, every time Swami visits the hospital, I am reminded of how fortunate we are—the Lord Himself is coming to us; we do not even have to go to Him to have His holy *darshan*. What better boon could we ask from Him?

The next day, while sitting for morning *darshan*, I was praying for my father who was not well. Swami came and stood directly in front of me. I informed Him of my father's condition and he materialized a beautiful silver ring. Putting it in my shirt pocket, He told me to send it to my father. Then, in a low tone, He said that several dignitaries and officials were waiting for His *darshan*. I felt so humble and blessed that Swami came to me that day.

For the next several days, Swami would speak to me daily—either in *darshan* line or in the interview room. On November 29th, He called Dr. P. Venugopal, Head of the Cardio-Thoracic Surgery Department at the All India Institute of Medical Sciences, and the rest of his team from Delhi. They were the ones performing the majority of operations at our Institute. Swami was kind enough to call me also with them.

In this interview, the number and variety of articles that Swami materialized was mind boggling. First, He produced a charming Seiko International golden watch for one of the men present. Turning to the doctors present, Swami, with one wave of His hand, materialized seven gold rings with *navratnas* studded on them. Swami personally slipped a ring onto the finger of each doctor; an exact fit for each of us. He then distributed rich, woolen suit pieces and shawls to each of us. Swami Himself selected the color that would suit me. He placed one against my face and said "No." He selected another color and did not approve of that one either. Finally, He was satisfied with the third one, saying: "Yes, this will suit your color." (Right from the beginning when I saw the bunch of suit pieces, this was the color that I wanted for myself.)

After distributing shawls and silk saris to the ladies present, Swami looked at me and asked: "What is the meaning of Venugopal?" I replied: "Bhagawan, 'venu' means flute and 'gopal' means Krishna. So Venugopal means Krishna with the flute." Swami smiled and swirled His hand in the now familiar way, materializing a *navratna* necklace with a huge golden Lord Krishna hanging from the center. Lord Krishna was playing the flute, and Swami said: "Here is Venugopal." He passed it around before placing it around the neck of Dr. Venugopal. Still, His creations for that day were not finished. Swami then produced gold coins in His hand, giving one to each of about 25 ladies seated. When He finished, there were a few left in His hand. He opened His palm, and the gold melted right into His hand. This was the first time I had ever seen something being de-materialized by Swami. Not only can He create absolutely anything, living or inanimate, but He can de-materialize things as well. Finally, Swami waved His hand yet again, and simultaneously produced two Seiko ladies watches: one for their anesthetist, and the other for their senior-most nursing sister.

Swami knows everything about everyone. He knows who needs what and exactly when they need it. The day before this dazzling interview, we were having breakfast at the hospital, and one of the visiting doctors was speaking quite critically of Swami. I was feeling a little disturbed and said to her: "Madam, if you could experience even a little of what I have experienced with Swami, you would pronounce Him the *Avatar* of our age in one second. I am sure, that as soon as you meet Swami in that interview room, you will agree with me." She remained unconvinced. The next day during this interview, I found her weeping uncontrollably. I asked her why she was crying, and she replied: "Yes, doctor. He is God who knows everything." Within 24 hours, Swami had transformed her heart and instilled faith in her.

Before the interview was over, Swami got up and brought one more silk sari. He gave it to a lady who did not receive one earlier. He said: **"Awareness—Yes, I know she was left out before. Knowing everything totally, all the time, is awareness."** If we could attain a fraction of His awareness, there would be no conflict in the world today. See how carefully Swami teaches us by His own example.

A few days later, Sham told me that Bhagawan had informed Dr. Alreja (another elderly and respected doctor in Prasanthi Nilayam) that He is bringing one female dental surgeon here, and she happened to be the wife of the blood bank officer. As Sham narrated this to me, I could not curb my tears. I had just written a letter to Swami asking Him if he could bring Poonam and the children here, and that letter was still in my pocket. In addition, the previous day, Dr. Bhagwat, Medical Superintendent, casually asked me about my family. When I told him that my wife was a dental surgeon, he said that much before I even joined my post, Bhagawan had informed him that He would be bringing a lady dental surgeon here, so her post need not be advertised as He Himself will directly appoint her. Dr. Bhagwat told me that only now he understood that probably Swami had been referring to my wife. I felt so happy at the thought of our family being reunited.

That evening during *darshan*, Swami slowly walked over to me. As I stood with folded hands, He reached into my shirt pocket and said: "Keeping wife in pocket." I answered: "No, Bhagawan, only you. Here, as well as in my heart." Swami glanced at me with a bewitching smile and pulled out the letter from my pocket. He said: "What is this—wife?" I could not figure out what He was talking about. On seeing the letter requesting Him to bring Poonam here, I was reminded: "Oh, Bhagawan, yes." He nodded, saying: "Yes, yes. I know, I know wife is a dental surgeon." And He walked away.

The next day Swami came out of His room and said: "Your wife is a dentist." I replied: "Yes Swami." He said: "Call her." A few days later, Swami called me for an interview and inquired about my wife and children. He told me to get my daughters' transfer certificates, and He would give them admission in His school. Accordingly, I called my wife and asked them all to come. Over the next several days, Swami repeatedly asked me about my family. Each time I called Abohar telling them to come quickly.

One day, Swami called a group of His students from the Anantapur campus whom He had selected to be nurses in the hospital. They were to travel to Delhi to receive their training. Swami gave each of them a woolen blanket, spending money, and other instructions about maintaining high standards of character and morality. It appeared as if the Divine Mother was affectionately guiding and protecting Her little daughters. With the wave of His hand Swami materialized a beautiful silver locket for each girl. Then He produced a *Shiva Lingam* which He told them to always keep with them and perform *Abhishekam* of it daily. Drinking that water would protect them from all diseases on their journey.

On December 11th, I went to Dharmavaram station to receive my family. It was a joyous reunion after a separation of about one-and-a-half months. We all had dreams and hopes for our new life at Bhagawan's Lotus Feet. During evening *darshan* Swami came to me and asked about their arrival. I told Him that they had arrived, and He said: "Yes I can tell from your face that wife has come. There is a glow on your face." I just blushed and fell at His feet. Then Swami said: "Wife is there (pointing towards the ladies' side where Poonam was sitting), but LIFE is here (pointing to Himself)." I said: "Yes, Swami everything is here." Swami, You are our anchor. We have left everything in Abohar only at Your command. We see before us a vast ocean of Your Divine Grace. Please! Always keep us here at Your feet.

For two days Swami did not call us for interview. We were growing anxious because with each passing day, the girls were missing school. Intensely, each of us prayed to Bhagawan to guide us as to our future course. Finally, on December 13, 1991, Swami told me to call my family. They all came rushing from the ladies' side. In the interview room, Swami introduced me as His blood bank officer, and Poonam as His dental surgeon. He called my younger daughter, Rachita, toward Him and asked her name. She replied: "Rachita." With a wave of His hand, Swami materialized a beautiful heart-shaped silver locket with His bust in gold embossed on the front and gave it to her. A moment later He took it back asking her: "Where is your chain? How will you put it around your neck?" Then He held the locket in His hand and blew on it three times. There appeared a beautiful silver chain with the locket hanging on it. With His own hands, He tied it around her neck.

In the inner interview room, Swami loved us so much. He told my wife about her father's death. Poonam took his death very hard as she is the eldest child. Patting her, Swami said: "Don't worry. From today, Swami is your Father, and you are my daughter. Ask anything you want from me." Emotions caused us all to choke up. Poonam could not utter a word.

Swami asked my elder daughter Shweta what she would like to become. She answered: "Doctor, Swami." Baba said: "Yes, become a doctor—not a dental doctor like mother, but a gynecologist. Do your M.B.B.S., but don't stop there, as M.B.B.S. is only an intermediate. Swami will give you admission in Bangalore Medical College and then make you a gynecologist, after which He will send you to London for doing higher studies. Swami will spend 5 lakh rupees on your education. Then, He will give you a job in His hospital." Turning to Rachita, he asked her what she would like to become. She said: "Swami, not a doctor." Baba said: "Yes, yes. Not doctor. You will be an I.A.S. (Indian Administrative Service) Officer. Start hard work from now." As my wife and I listened to all this, we felt an enormous sense of gratitude towards Swami. He had taken from us the burden of raising our children and settling them in life.

After seeing the previous records and certificates of the girls, Swami told us that He would speak to the headmistress of His school to admit our daughters on Monday. He told Poonam to join as dental surgeon after Makara-Sankranthi as that would be a very auspicious time for her. Fully contented, we moved out of the room.

On Saturday, December 14, Swami called us again along with Dr. Safaya, Dr. Bhagwat, Dr. Hary, Mrs. Parvati Ram, Nursing Superintendent, and her four daughters. He materialized three lockets on chains for Mrs. Ram's three youngest daughters. For the eldest daughter, Swami made a beautiful pair of earrings in the shape of an "S". Shweta began to cry silently. Swami asked her: "Why are you weeping? Because Swami gave locket to other sister that day and not to you. Feeling jealous?" There moved the Divine hand and appeared a beautiful locket on a chain, similar to the one given to Rachita. In the inner interview room, Bhagawan told us to take our daughters to the school on Monday after 9 a.m. as from 7.30 a.m. to 9 a.m., it was an inauspicious time.

Swami meticulously takes care of the smallest details.

The next day, I went to the hospital and came to know that Swami was coming to visit. Since I was the only doctor present, I rushed to receive Him. He visited each department and went upstairs in the elevator. I received the rare opportunity of being alone with Swami in the lift. As it moved up, I silently prayed: "Lord, continue lifting me spiritually as well as physically so that I can exist in a state where nothing remains except You." Before leaving the hospital, Swami gave His blessings and most sought after *padnamaskar*.

On Monday, December 16, 1991, at 9:30 a.m. Poonam and I took Shweta and Rachita to the greatest educational institution on Earth, the one that is continuously being blessed by God Himself. This school that would one day be their alma mater, was going to shape their lives, their careers, their destinies, and fortunes. The headmistress, Ms. Munni Kaul, lovingly took our girls in her lap, and assured us of their care. After leaving them, I became extremely emotional and the tears flowed—tears of separation, tears of joy, tears of gratitude towards Bhagawan. Parents yearn and pray for years together for their children to be admitted in Swami's school. How could we ever repay Him?

The next day, Swami called me in for an interview, and He announced that it was a very auspicious day: Vaikunta Ekadasi, the day that Lord Vishnu distributed *amritha* to all the gods and goddesses. I was sitting there in the Sai Vaikunta and Sai Vishnu was in front of us, blessing us all. Among us, there was a lady from Malaysia who was the headmistress of a music school, General Carlos, the ex-president of Guatemala, his wife and granddaughter, Dr. Safaya, and Dr. Bhagwat. Swami again went on a materializing spree. He made a lovely pair of peacock-shaped earrings for the headmistress, an extraordinary golden statue of Goddess Lakshmi for Mrs. Carlos, a unique pair of earrings for their granddaughter. Those earrings had a star, with a heart attached to the star by means of a hook. Swami told her: "This is Swami's Christmas gift to her. The Christmas Star is being given to her." He explained the significance; the heart was the jivi or the individual soul, the star was the Paramatma, or Universal soul, the hook was the means to always remain attached. The individual should always remain attached to God.

Then Swami informed us about various aspects of the hospital. He told us how doctors should deal with patients, and other things. Each word of His is full of Divine wisdom and carries its message directly to one's heart. There, the message gets imprinted and slowly starts changing your attitude day by day.

Swami asked me about the children's entrance in school. I told Him that we left them the previous day. He knew the pain that I had in my heart due to the sudden separation from the children. He told me not to worry at all; Baba would take care of them. In my heart, I said to Him we have placed ourselves at Your Lotus Feet; whatsoever You do, we will take it as Your grace. "We have come this far only by Your blessings, otherwise we would have become lost in the mundane and materialistic world long ago."

When the Lord wishes to shower His grace, it is overflowing. One day I was sitting in the verandah when Swami called me forward to ask about our daughters' adjustment to hostel life. He reassured me and gave me *padnamaskar*. After *darshan*, He again spoke to me, giving me a book and *padnamaskar*. He went into His room and returned, asking me some details about the hospital, and He bestowed *padnamaskar* once again. He returned to His room, emerged, gave me another book, and *padnamaskar* for the fourth time in one morning. How blessed and lucky are His devotees.

Swami asked us to go to Punjab to wind up our affairs and to return soon. Accordingly, on December 28, 1991, Poonam and I left for Punjab. Upon reaching Abohar, we vacated the government house that had been given to us and disposed of the majority of our household articles as directed by Swami. The whole trip was very hectic and full of emotion. We were bidding good-bye to the place that had become the center of our lives in so many ways for so many years. Actually, we had become a part of the life of Abohar. Every brick and every stone seemed to be asking me why I was leaving, what was lacking in Abohar that I had to leave so abruptly? Abohar had been my "karma bhoomi", the place that gave me the opportunity to work in a manner that ultimately took me to the Divine Lotus Feet of the Lord. That alone would be my permanent abode now. Dear friends and loved ones gathered at the railway station when we left. Every eye had tears, and I, of course, was the first to break down.

We returned to Prasanthi on January 7th. Swami asked me: "When did you come?" I answered: "Today." He said: "Yes, I know. You have come along with your wife—life. I saw her sitting on that side. It is written on your face."

The next day, I received my first paycheck as Divine blessings. I was also given some photographs taken when Bhagawan visited the blood bank in November. I wanted to offer the very first check to Bhagawan, but was feeling a bit hesitant. There are so many devotees that offer lakhs and crores at His feet, and often He does not accept. I felt like the small squirrel who brought a few dust particles on her body to the ocean. She takes a dip, hoping and praying that that sand may also be accepted by Lord Rama in the construction of the bridge over the sea to Lanka. Those prayers were arising in my heart. The check was in an envelope in my shirt pocket. Swami called me in and pulled it out of my pocket, asking: "What is this?" I replied: "Swami, it is nothing." He then said: **"For me, nothing is everything, and everything is nothing."** Then I said: "Swami, these are just a few drops of Your mercy. Let them merge back into Your vast ocean, and let me feel that vastness." He patted me and graciously accepted the envelope. It is only when an individual drop loses its identity that it can merge into the vast ocean.

Both Poonam and I were anxiously awaiting the official starting of her duty, but we had no sign from Bhagawan. I asked Him about it on January 13th, and His reply was: "I will see." Makara-Sankranthi arrived on the 15th, and both of us were on pins and needles, waiting for the news. At noon, Colonel Joga Rao Ji met me, giving me the happy news. Swami had asked him to convey to my wife and me that Poonam should join on that day as Swami's dental surgeon in the General Hospital. I offered millions of salutations at the Lotus Feet.

Actually, the events went something like this. Swami was going somewhere in His car, when He stopped and said something to Col. Joga Rao Ji referring to Sham who was nearby. Sham became nervous, wondering what Swami was saying. Col. Joga Rao Ji then went to Sham's room, inquiring about me and passing on the good news. Both Sham and Usha were so happy that they rushed to our room to tell Poonam. I learned about it a little later when I came home from the hospital for lunch.

The next day, Swami asked me about Poonam joining duty. He said a new dental chair unit had arrived, and I should help in getting it installed. After *darshan,* He returned and told me that He had called my wife for an interview. I rushed into the room as well. Swami introduced both of us to the other devotees assembled there. Then He asked Poonam what she wanted. She prayerfully kept quiet. Swami moved His hand and produced a huge lump of something white and soft. He handed it to her saying: "Dental Surgeon, you stop other people from taking sweet things, here Swami gives you sweet." It was a sugar candy that slowly hardened and became transparent. In the inner room, Swami profusely blessed both of us and promised to always take care of us and to keep us in the ashram only. He took a small photograph of Him from my hand and wrote: "To Nareshee" on it, instructing me to keep it always with me. Swami again told us that we should get the dental chair installed and then He would personally come to inaugurate it.

Swami called me in along with Dr. Safaya, Dr. Bhagwat, and Dr. Kanetkar. He asked me how much salary I was receiving at my previous post. The salary I was getting at SSSIHMS was not even half the salary of my earlier one, but I had not come to Swami for money. Money had never been an aim in my life. Anyone would tell you that Dr. Bhatia never accepted a penny from any patient, or for that matter, from anyone. I did not say anything. Swami repeated His question. I told Him that whatever I received would be His *prasad* and carried His blessings. However, Swami knew my financial obligations, particularly the repayment of the housing loan that we took for building our bungalow. Bhagawan instructed Dr. Safaya to increase my salary to more than the amount I received at my previous position. Swami said that He knew we had hardly any bank balance, with two daughters to educate, get married, etc. I never worried about such things. When Swami is present, we do not need anything else.

On January 20, 1992, Swami went to the General Hospital to inaugurate the new dental unit. He posed for photographs with Poonam. Then, He came to our hospital and asked why I was not present because He wanted to take pictures with both of us. He scolded me like a mother; His love is infinite.

On the 21st, Swami left for Bombay to celebrate the 25th anniversary of Dharmakshetra there. It was the first time that I had to bid Swami farewell. This separation was much more bitter than ones in the past. As any resident in Prasanthi will tell you, everything seems lifeless when Swami is away. Anxiously, we awaited His return until on February 7th, life began afresh when Bhagawan came back to Prasanthi.

Swami visited the hospital soon after He came back from Bombay. I happened to be the only doctor on hand, and I met Him at the gate. Swami rarely wears *chappals*, but on this day, He was lifting a pair from His car. Immediately, I rushed forward to take them from Him, and place them on the ground, helping Him wear them. I felt so blessed to touch those *padukas;* I imagined how Bharata felt when Lord Rama gave His *padukas* to Bharata. Lord, You know what I was when You were Rama, but I know only one thing since time immemorial: I LOVE YOU, I LOVE YOU, I LOVE YOU.

A few days later, Swami called a man "from Paris" for an interview. Subsequently, we learned that he was actually a Count of Paris. Later, he and his wife came to visit the hospital and were duly impressed by its grandeur. The Count then showed me a ring with the portrait of Jesus Christ that Swami materialized for him. On February 14, 1992, we were informed that Prince Charles, heir to the throne of England would be coming to visit the hospital as he was keen on seeing it after hearing so much about it. Due to security reasons, his trip was postponed, but later I came to know that he had written a very fine letter expressing his genuine desire to see the hospital and meet Swami.

Continuing on the line of prominent dignitaries and heads of state, the Vice-President of India, Dr. S.D. Sharma, and the Speaker of Lok Sabha, Shri Shiv Raj Patil and their families, came to seek Baba's blessings and visited the hospital. When they came to the blood bank, Swami introduced me by saying: "He is Dr. Bhatia, My Blood Bank Officer. He is from Punjab. His wife is a dentist, and she, too, has been appointed by Swami in the General Hospital." On a lighter note, I said: "Sir, Swami has picked up a terrorist from Punjab. They take blood with bullets, but I am taking it in bags." Swami was quite amused. I said to Him: "Swami, today is the most fortunate day for Indian democracy." He asked me: "How?" I replied: "Swami, as both the Chairman of the Rajaya Sabha and the Speaker of the Lok Sabha are at Your Divine Lotus Feet seeking blessings, the entire nation is represented and is receiving Your Grace." Swami smiled very sweetly at me.

Nearly everyday, Swami would ask either Poonam or me how we were, how the children were, how our respective duties were coming along. Like a caring and devoted parent, He attended to our every need and want. One day, Swami came and distributed calculators to Dr. Safaya, Dr. Bhatt, and Dr. Bhagwat. He also gave me one saying: "Take Blood Bank. Calculate the amount of bottles." I continued feeling His love and affection for a long time after that.

February 27th was Rachita's birthday. For the first time, she was not at home but in the hostel. Naturally, we missed her, but at the same time we were happy that she was in Swami's fold. I recollected everything about Rachita—from the time she was growing in her mother's womb to her birth, and all the wonderful memories after that. Really, she was the one who brought us to Swami first in 1981. The school children are brought for *darshan* on Thursdays and Sundays. As her birthday happened to be on a Thursday, she had come and was allowed to sit in the first row. Swami accepted a rose from her, conveying His blessings and acceptance of her. I prayed to Bhagawan to bless this doll whom He had sent to our family for spreading her joy to all.

The morning after Maha Shivaratri, Swami supervised the distribution of prasad to all 40,000 people assembled in the Poornachandra Auditorium. He saw me and lovingly asked me to eat. The Divine Mother is ever-watchful of her little children. Once, in *darshan* line, Swami said to my wife: "Dental Surgeon, when you have no other work, pull out the teeth of your husband." One of the technicians of my department was seated next to her, and Swami told Poonam to pull out that girl's teeth as well. The Lord conveys His love and energy through these small conversations.

On March 6, 1992, Swami was to leave Puttaparthi for Whitefield. We were all filled with deep sadness for this upcoming separation. As His car passed the hospital, Swami waved to all of us. Seeing me standing with my eyes full of tears, Swami stretched His hand out the window and took my hand in His, conveying that He would always hold me, even when not physically present. I bowed in reverence and kissed that hand.

On the 26th of that month, I decided to go to Whitefield to have our Lord's *darshan.* Swami called me and gave so much love. I told Him that this was my first visit to Whitefield, and like a proper host, He showed me everything in Trayee Brindavan, His abode. He asked about my family and again assured me that He had reserved a seat for Shweta in Bangalore Medical College. In the evening, Swami called me and asked: "Bhatia, have you seen my new car?" I replied: "No, Swami." Like a playful child, Swami showed me everything in His shining new Jaguar—the T.V., V.C.R., telephone, refrigerator and many other gadgets. I felt thrilled to be near Swami, and He was obviously enjoying. Then, He brought a huge bag with apples and sweets for us. It was really a most remarkable day.

A few days later, our family again went to Whitefield. I had arranged a blood donation camp, and 62 donors gave the gift of liquid love that day. My daughter Shweta had been suffering from leucoderma, a skin pigmentation disorder, since she was about seven. Swami told her to take B complex vitamins twice a day to relieve her condition. He told me not to go back but to stay in Whitefield overnight. On the one hand, duty was calling me; on the other hand Divinity was commanding me. Swami went upstairs and saw me from His balcony. He called: "Bhatia." I rushed up to Him, and He again told me to stay in Whitefield. I prayerfully said: "Swami, I must go, since the blood that I have collected must reach the hospital tonight for tomorrow's operations." Swami lovingly coaxed me: "Don't go. Stay. Go early in the morning at 5 o'clock." The Omniscient One knew all that I did not, but I persisted in my endeavor. I pleaded with Him, and He reluctantly gave me permission to go. We reached the hospital at about 11:30 p.m., and then I came to know that all the operations scheduled for that day were postponed because the first case of the day had developed complications and the surgeons were busy with that patient all day. Blood had already been arranged for the other cases, so I could have stayed in Whitefield overnight. Swami played a Divine *leela* with me.

When Swami returned from Kodaikanal, I went to Whitefield to have *darshan*. In the evening, Swami called the staff members of the hospital that were present for an interview. Inside, he performed the marriage of Dr. T. Nandapal, Professor of Radiology in Hyderabad. Swami materialized a diamond ring for the wife to slip on the finger of her husband and a beautiful gold necklace for the husband to tie around his wife's neck. He also made a gold *mangal sutra* for her. After blessing them both, Swami said: "See Bhatia, Swami has to act as a priest as well." Swami gave them blessings and wedding gifts. He said that their elderly mother was Swami's devotee for the last fifty years.

On another day when we had gone to Whitefield, my sister Meenakshi accompanied us because her children were seeking admission in Swami's school in the tenth and eighth class. Within a week, we received the joyous news that both her son and her daughter had been granted admission after passing the entrance exams.

On June 6, 1992, we learned that Swami was returning to Prasanthi Nilayam. All the agonizing prayers and throbbing hearts must have moved Him to come to us. Our faces were filled with a different radiance that day. The expectation and anticipation of the arrival of our Lord could not be hidden. As His car passed us, it appeared as if my heart had stopped beating for a few seconds. The desire to see Swami gradually transformed into a feeling of tranquility.

The next day after morning *darshan*, I continued sitting in the verandah. Swami came out after giving interviews and said: "Sitting here? No work in the hospital?" I humbly replied that since the bus for the hospital did not leave until 8:30, I would have a chance for another glimpse of my Lord. He lovingly patted me and said: "Eight-thirty, eight-thirty, eight-thirty." He granted me a most loving *padnamaskar* and told me He would speak to us.

In the evening, Swami told me to call my wife. I stood in the verandah facing the ladies' side and searched the crowd. For a few seconds, I could not find her. Then, she saw me and came running. In the inner room, Swami once again assured us of Shweta's admission in Bangalore Medical College and accommodation in the ashram. Swami scolded me for being harsh toward my wife and told me to shed my anger. Poonam told Him that I was shedding it slowly. Swami took His handkerchief in His hand and threw it saying: "All bad habits should be discarded in one stroke, and good habits should be acquired and developed slowly." I told Swami about the admission of my niece and nephew in Swami's school. He said: "Who gave them admission? I gave them. They came last year and in the interview room, Swami told them to apply here, and they would be admitted. Then you requested me the same in Whitefield. Isn't it? I know, I know. I remember." I said: "Yes, Swami. It all happened exactly as You said."

Swami scolded me, asking why I praise Him so much. I talked about Him too much on my vacation in Punjab; I went to Anantapur and gave lectures. Swami said He does not need any advertisement. I told Him that as His humble servant, I never speak too much. This limited mind cannot adequately discuss the Unlimited, the boundless. I only try to glorify the Divinity of Swami and to truthfully narrate what I have experienced.

We learned that Swami was going back to Whitefield the next day, and our hearts were filled with sadness. Before leaving, He called me along with the Vice-Chancellor and Registrar of the University and instructed me to go to the boys' hostel for one hour every evening to attend to any boys that fall sick. Lovingly, He blessed us and left.

Swami returned to us again on July 2, 1992. On the 7th, Swami called me in the verandah and spoke to me for about 20-25 minutes about hospital affairs. He told me that I was a 100% liar and a cheat because I never tell him anything that is happening in the hospital. I said: "Bhagawan, what can I tell You when You know everything, and how can my little judgment stand before Your Divine judgment? I have no right to judge others' actions. I can only watch my own." Swami lovingly snubbed me and gave me the example of Lord Rama who deputed Samantha to relay information. It was only Samantha's report that led to Sita's exile. During this period, Swami gave me *padnamaskar* four times. I only prayed to Him: Lord, let the seed of Thy Divine Love sown in my heart one day blossom into a beautiful rose of Love.

July 8th was our wedding anniversary. Swami came to me and said: "Birthday today." I kept quiet. He changed His mind: "No, wedding day today. How many years?" I replied: "Swami, eighteen years." He laughed and asked: "Eighteen years? You don't look eighteen years old married man." Bhagawan, everything is Your grace. Do You look 67 years old? Baba continued: "How many children?" "Swami, two daughters." He said: "No, eighteen daughters." He smiled, giving me *padnamaskar* before walking away. After returning from *darshan*, Swami gestured for me to call my wife for interview. In the inner room, Swami suddenly remarked: "Ayio! I forgot to bring gift!" He moved out, and we could hear Him opening a steel cupboard. He returned with a lovely blue colored (my favorite color) sari for Poonam. Handing it to her, He said: "Pure kanjivaram silk. Costs Rs. 3,000." And He showed us the price tag.

Swami asked us how long we had been married. I told Him eighteen years. "What is the significance of the number 18?" He asked. I replied: "Swami eight plus one is nine, the Divine number. The *Geeta* has eighteen chapters; the Mahabharata battle lasted eighteen days; In that, eighteen *Kshoni* army were killed;" He asked: "What more?" I answered: "Swami, we have eighteen *puranas*." "What more?" He questioned. Then my Krishna Himself declared: "Krishna had eighteen chariots." He then asked Poonam and I to keep our heads on His Lotus Feet together and blessed us both. As I looked up at Him, my eyes were wet with tears. Swami asked: "Why do you weep?" I responded: "Swami they are tears of love for You." He said: "Yes, I know you LOVE me. I also LOVE you."

I asked Bhagawan to grant me three promises that day. Baba said: "Yes, what?" I began: "Swami, first let this LOVE flow between You and me for eternity. If there is a break for even a fraction of a second, let that be my last moment." Swami agreed and asked for the second. I said: "Bhagawan, I cannot live without You anywhere anymore. Please always, always, always keep me in Your Divine Lotus Feet here only." Swami granted me that second promise as well. Finally, He said: "What is the third?" With the utmost humility and devotion, I requested: "Swami, please personally receive me at the end of my journey." My Beloved Lord put His hand in my tiny hand and said: "Promise, I will do that. I will personally receive You at the end. Don't worry. Don't cry."

Then Swami said to me: "I know you are sad today." I said: "No, Swami." He repeated His sentence and added:

"Yes, it is your family's happy occasion. Today, daughters should have also been there with you. Isn't it? Why did you not tell me yesterday? I would have called them also for interview. Don't worry. Tomorrow, I will again call. Be happy. Be prepared for tomorrow." Then we emerged. After introducing us to everyone in the outer interview room, Swami allowed us to have our photograph taken with Him. Really, these are precious moments that we will always treasure.

Before the interview was over, Swami made me and my wife stand up, and He announced: "My blood bank doctor, my dental surgeon. Their wedding anniversary today. Swami will celebrate." He waved His hand and produced *"burfi"*, a sweet made from milk. He distributed the *burfi* to all present; there must have been more than one kilogram of *burfi* flowing from the Divine hands! As we left the interview room, Swami said: "Be ready for tomorrow."

During evening bhajans, Swami came out of the *mandir* and called me: "Bhatia." I rushed to him. He whispered very softly into my ear: "Bhatia, not tomorrow. I have called M.B.A. students." I said: "O.K. Swami." He said: "No. While sitting in bhajan, Swami got worried that you will wait for tomorrow." How loving and thoughtful were those words. Swami, please, don't worry for this child of yours. *Your Love is sufficient to sustain me in my life. Your wish is my command.* Swami continued: "Don't worry, Sunday I will call."

Sunday arrived, but I was hesitant. A sweet and loving boy named Dilip, who looks after Swami's personal room, said to me: "Sir, today is Sunday." I told him: "Dilip, I know. But only Swami knows to which Sunday he is referring." So many times, Swami gives a date or a time, but it does not immediately materialize. His ways can only be described as Divine. But, Swami did call our whole family in for an interview. After asking Poonam what she wanted, He waved His hand, materializing a diamond ring for her. He showed it to all of us and then asked her: "Do you want a diamond

144

ring or *navratna,* as given to husband?" He proceeded to change the diamond ring into the exactly same as the one I received in November, 1991. Slipping it onto her finger, Swami said: "Now you won't fight. Both are given similar rings." Poonam was really thrilled. In the inner interview room, Swami repeated His promise to make Shweta a doctor. He told her to become a child specialist. Swami, it is only Your grace that will make her become anything.

One day, Swami was distributing handkerchiefs with "S's" embroidered on them. When He came to me, he asked me: "What is your name?" I replied: "Naresh, Swami." He looked in His basket: "No hanky with 'N'." Another time, I was sitting next to Mr. Oberoi who is looking after the airport. It was his birthday. Swami stood before him and said: "Keeping wife in pocket." Mr. Oberoi was confused. Swami turned to me and asked: "Isn't it? He keeps his wife in his pocket." Laughing like a small child with a secret, Swami walked away. How He loves to play games with His devotees!

My wife's birthday was approaching, and I was waiting for a chance to tell Swami. He came near, and I stood up: "Swami, wife's birthday tomorrow." Swami pretended not to hear: "What?" I repeated: "Swami, wife's birthday." He smiled and said: "Why are you so worried if it is her birthday?" He gave me *padnamaskar* and moved on. The next day, Swami called Poonam out of *darshan* line on her birthday and said: "Birthday yesterday," blessing her with *padnamaskar* and materialized vibhuti.

Once, my wife's cousins were coming in connection with the admission of one of their daughters in a college in Bangalore. I told Swami: "Wife's cousins have come." Swami looked at me and said: "One marriage not sufficient. Want one more." I became perplexed by this statement and wondered about it for a long time. Only He knows His mysterious ways. He continued standing in front of me for about fifteen minutes, and I had the privilege of doing *pad seva*, pressing the Lotus Feet. Swami blessed me profusely, and before leaving He said: "Om Shanti, Shanti, Shanti."

Bhagawan then put me through a test. After receiving so much LOVE from Him, I tasted the bitterness of His silence as well. Days passed without even a glance from Him. The pangs that I felt in my heart manifested themselves in my eyes. Tears flowed like rivers, but my Lord was unmoved. While sitting for *darshan*, poetry would pour out of me. The child was crying out for its share of food from Mother.

On Janamashtami, as the college boys presented their enchanting music program, I became lost in my Krishna. I remembered the days when He would come to me and love me—His *gopika*, His Radha. I longed to be back in those blissful days. All these sentiments were being noted down, when I realized my Beloved Sai Krishna was actually standing before me. His eyes pierced into my soul. I became absorbed in peering into THOSE EYES that watched and conveyed everything. Although I felt the love emanating from Him, He still did not speak a word.

My sister and her husband had come from Hyderabad, and Swami called me to inquire about them. The silence was broken at last! He told me to call my nephew and daughters the next day, September 1, 1992. With our hearts throbbing in anticipation, we all sat for *darshan* the next day. Swami pointed to my nephew to call his sister and parents. Our family was not summoned. With heavy hearts, we watched them enter the interview room. Our daughters burst into tears at not being called. Inside, Swami blessed my sister by producing a Shiva *Lingam* for her and a ring for her son.

The next week, my eldest brother came, and Swami asked me to "Call brother." Then He told me to call Udit, our nephew. The three of us were going in when Swami instructed me to sit out. I was surprised, but since I had no choice, I sat outside. A little while later, Swami emerged and called me: "Where is the other nephew?" Confused, I said: "Swami, only one nephew." He said: "No, I saw the other nephew sitting in the hall." Swami entered the *mandir*, and called Pankaj, Sham's wife Usha's nephew. Swami asked me: "Isn't he your nephew?" I replied: "Swami, Sham's." Then Swami questioned me: "No, his mother is your sister, isn't it?" I thought to myself, why let this boy lose the chance of getting an interview, so I said: "Yes." Swami led us both toward His room, and then told me to go back and sit. Silently, I obeyed and sat down, praying. Inside, Basant *Bhayya* received Swami's robe and Pankaj got a beautiful ring with Baby Krishna on it. Swami blessed three of my photos, so in this way, I, too, received His blessings.

I continued praying to my Lord to melt His heart. He even stopped coming to the hospital, so those wonderful experiences ended also. Introspectively, I searched my heart, but found only Love for Bhagawan emanating in all directions. I could only wait for things to unfold.

On September 27, 1992, I had a dream in which Swami came and was knocking at my door. I loudly said: "Coming, Swami," and waking up, I jumped out of bed to open the door. The time was 1 a.m., and who did I find at the door, but my sister Meenakshi and her husband. They were holding a beautiful photograph of Swami that He had earlier blessed. They got the picture laminated and brought it to me on my birthday. Before sleeping, I had prayed to Swami that I should see His face as soon as I wake up in the morning. My sister and her husband were supposed to arrive by bus at 6 a.m., but they decided to travel by taxi all night and reach early. After 22 years, my twin sister and I were celebrating OUR birthday together, and most auspiciously at our Lord's Divine Feet. Swami called us all for an interview that morning and blessed us so much. All of our children were also present, and Swami graciously agreed to so many photographs with our families. They will form permanent memories of ours with the Divine.

Months passed in the bliss of being in the Divine presence. On March 3, 1993, Swami came to me in the verandah and asked: "Are you coming?" I asked Him: "Where, Swami?" He replied: "College Auditorium." I again asked: "When, Swami?" He answered: "Tomorrow morning at 7:30." He was inviting us to witness the farewell to Professor S. Sampath as Vice-Chancellor and the welcome to the new V.C., Professor Hanumanthappa.

Both Prof. Sampath, and the Registrar of the Institute, Mr. Chakravarthi, are noble people. I have had the privilege of working with both of them in connection with my work at the boys' hostel. They have always exemplified the ideals of Swami's goals in education. I have great admiration for them and their wives who have dedicated everything at Swami's Lotus Feet.

The ceremony the following day was very moving. Prof. Sampath was a figure of utmost humility and love. Swami graciously presented him with two gold *kangans* and *angavastram* and his wife with a beautiful sari. Entrusted with the responsibility of carrying out the duties of Vice-Chancellor, Prof. Hanumanthappa then took office.

A couple of days later, Swami came into the verandah and started distributing calculators to the doctors working in His hospital. I did not receive one, and some of the other doctors asked me about it. I told them that I really did not mind, for Swami knows His plan best. The next day, Swami continued passing on calculators, and I received three that day. When one is patient, He grants everything in plenty.

On March 7, 1993, my sister and her family came to Prasanthi Nilayam. Swami called them in for interviews on the 7th and 8th. He gave them His robes, a watch to my brother-in-law, a watch to my nephew, and a diamond ring to my sister. We all felt so happy that Swami bestowed His grace on them.

On the 8th, Col. Joga Rao Ji called me to the Director's office, and there I was informed that I was to look after the administration of the hospital in Dr. Safaya's absence. With all humility and devotion, I prayed to Swami to guide me in this task. That evening, Swami came to me and asked: "How is brother-in-law?" I answered: "Swami, must be happy." He asked me: "Did you meet him and see all that I gave?" I said: "No, Swami." He exclaimed: "Why? Swami gave them so many things." I said: "Swami, I just met him for a minute this morning before leaving for the hospital, and I am returning from there just now." Swami blessed me profusely and moved on. After a few minutes, He returned and asked me: "How is the hospital, sir?" I replied: "Bhagawan, the responsibility you have so mercifully given me is too big for a small person like me. Swami, You please take care of me. You have to do the work. I seek Your blessings." He gave me His blessings—a big thump on the back and *padnamaskar.*

On March 9, 1993, as I sat for morning *darshan*, I was feeling extremely peaceful. Swami pointed toward me and called us for an interview. In the inner room, Swami again reassured us about Shweta's admission in medical college. Then, He turned to me and said: "Bhatia, Dr. Safaya has gone on leave, Dr. Alreja is also going. You have to be the Acting Director for Superspecialty Hospital and General Hospital Incharge." I said: "Swami, there are so many other elder doctors. Please give them this responsibility. They are much better." Swami looked deep into me and said: "I have faith in you." Hearing these words from the Divine mouth, I fell at His feet, uttering: "Swami, please give me the strength to carry out this task, as without You, I cannot even breathe." Swami lovingly took my hand in His and said: "I will be with you, within you, around you. Don't worry. I will take care of everything."

Then Swami asked my younger daughter: "Where is your brother?" She was confused. He repeated the question three or four times. He looked at me with a mischievous smile and said: "Father knows. He wants a son. I will give him." Shweta shook her head in disagreement, and Swami said to her: "You keep quiet." Then, He again asked Rachita: "Where is brother? What is His name?" Rachita answered: "Udit." Swami said: "No, not Udit. He is your uncle's son. I am asking about your own real brother from this father." Only Swami understands His mysterious ways.

Swami scolded me, saying I did not sleep enough. He said that sometimes I wake up even as early as 2:30 a.m. Swami told me to sleep more, that it is important to have proper sleep. Throughout, He continued holding my hand in His, stroking it. My Sai Ma is ever merciful. We then moved to the outer room, after taking Bhagawan's blessings. There He looked at Shweta and materialized a beautiful golden Citizen watch. He put it around her wrist Himself and declared her to be His doctor. Swami looked at me and said: "Hey, how you look at me. Do you want to eat me? Come, eat. Eat me." I prostrated at Swami's Lotus Feet and washed them with my tears.

Baba showers this ash (*Vibhuthi*) from His palm, His forhead, His feet and His pictures. For His devotees, this gift of ash is the penance for all physical, mental and intellectual illness. Baba is indeed *Maheswara*.

"Sathya Sai"

Chapter 18

Festivals in Prasanthi Nilayam

Although every day is a festival in the presence of the Divine, there are some specific days and dates that mark holidays. India is a country rich in tradition and heritage. Each state has its own unique culture that it nourishes in addition to that developed by the nation as a whole. Since the *Avatar* has taken birth in south India, naturally, He celebrates those festivals of His native area. But Bhagawan is not limited to only Telugu holidays or even only to Indian holidays. He is the Father of all mankind.

Having been fortunate enough to come and live at the Divine Lotus Feet since November, 1991, I have seen the full year of festivals being celebrated in Prasanthi Nilayam. They remind us of the unity of religions and the truly secularistic culture of the Divine Abode. I thought it might be of some interest to readers to learn about the various occasions that are celebrated here.

Swami marks the new year of the English calendar, January 1st, by bestowing His blessings on people all over the world. New Year's Day is always an auspicious time, no matter when one celebrates the new year, and Bhagawan graciously imparts the Divine *amritha*, His discourse to all of us. Shortly thereafter, on the 11th of January, the annual Sports and Cultural Meet takes place. The students of Swami's colleges and schools, the Sri Sathya Sai Institute of Higher Learning perform breathtaking stunts and elaborate displays of song, dance, and theater. At each and every festival, these dedicated and loving students fill our hearts with joy by presenting a fantastic music program in the Divine presence.

Makara Sankranthi/Pongal also falls in the month of January. It marks the reaping of the harvest in southern India. Crops are harvested at this time, and the people of this area give their thanks to the Almighty Lord for His bounty. Swami gives a Divine discourse for all to enjoy and imbibe.

Maha Shivaratri usually comes in February or March. This is the night when the individual should remain awake to contemplate on the Higher Self. In years past, Swami used to perform vibhuti *abhishek*, or vibhuti bath of a silver statue of Shirdi Sai. From an empty vessel, Swami would make the vibhuti pour out onto the statue. He also used to produce a *Shiva Lingam;* it would be created in Swami's body and emerge from His mouth, causing Him a great deal of pain. The *lingam* represents the entire universe, and its manifestation symbolizes the birth of the cosmos from the Divine womb. Since about 1977, Swami has stopped both the vibhuti *abhishek* and the *lingodhbhav.* He gives a Divine discourse, and as usual ends with a bhajan. His students pick up and continue singing bhajans until morning. Swami returns the next day to shower His devotees with another discourse and the distribution of *prasad.*

The most important festival of March/April is that of Ugadi. It is the new year for all Telugu-speaking people. In recent years, Swami has been in Whitefield for this holiday. During His discourse, Swami explains the significance of the events in the upcoming year. Ram Navami comes shortly after Ugadi. It is a day spent in remembering Lord Rama, celebrating the important events in His life and their inner significance.

May 6th is Easwaramma Day. On that day, devotees gather at the *samadhi* of Swami's parents to pay obeisance to the biological parents of the present Divine Incarnation. Feeding of the poor in large numbers also takes place on this day. At the end of June or the beginning of July is *Guru*

Purnima. The date varies as to when a full moon appears. On that day, all spiritual aspirants place their salutations at the feet of their guru. In this age, we are so fortunate, that the Divine has come to be our *Sadguru*. He Himself is the One to take us across this ocean of life to be merged in Him.

Krishna Janmashtami, celebrating the birth of Lord Krishna, usually comes in late August. A procession of cows is led from the dairy, Gokulum, to the Prasanthi *Mandir* compound. They are gaily decorated and brought to Swami. He personally feeds them, reminiscent of the days when Krishna played with his herd in Gokul. Shortly after, on Ganesh Chathurthi, a procession of devotees and students bear statues of Lord Ganesha. Usually, about three days later, these statues are immersed in water, in a nearby stream or well. It is said that Ganesha returns to His home by an underwater route.

The Kerala new year, Onam, is also at this time of year. It is associated with the Vamana *Avatar*. The Vamana *Avatar*, assuming the form of a young *sadhu*, asked King Bali, a virtuous and noble ruler, for land. The amount of land he requested would be measured in only three paces. Bali readily agreed to what he believed to be a mere three paces of land. Changing to a giant form, the Vamana covered the Earth in one step, the skies in the second. King Bali, realizing Divinity, offered his head as the third step. His story symbolizes the complete surrender of the individual in order to procure the Grace of the Lord.

In September/October comes Navratras with Vijaya Dashmi. This is a day to worship the Mother Goddesses: Durga, Lakshmi, and Saraswati, the embodiments of strength, prosperity, and knowledge, respectively. *Yajnas* are performed everyday for nine days by scholarly vedic pundits and priests. On the last day, Swami used to perform Poorna Ahuthi; he would materialize yellow rice and precious stones, *navratnas*, and throw them into the sacred fire. Vijaya Dashmi is the day when Rama defeated Ravana signifying the triumph of good over evil, virtue over vice. It is also simollanghan, which literally means "crossing the line", when the soul crosses its physical limits of the body. On this day, Shirdi Baba left His body.

Deepavali, the festival of light, comes in October on a new moon night. Swami distributes firecrackers to His students and even partakes in the lighting of them, bringing *ananda* to all those watching.

From November 19th to the 24th, festivities associated with Swami's birthday take place. The anniversary of His birth reminds us of the greatest event that has occurred in history: the advent of the *Avatar*, the Divine Incarnation. All of nature and mankind bow down before Divinity. Swami arrives in His chariot, with both hands raised in blessing. Thousands of poor people are fed and clothed by Bhagawan Himself. In the evening, there is a cultural program given by Swami's students and the Bal-Vikas children of nearby states. Every two years there is an All-India Conference, and every five years an international conference. Devotees gather to assess the progress taking place within the Sai Organization worldwide. On the day before Swami's birthday, the 22nd of November, the Convocation ceremony of the University takes place. Unlike other convocations, there are no special invitations, all are welcome. The Divine Chancellor bestows His blessings and awards degrees to the candidates. Now, November 22nd will also be the day for the celebration of the inauguration of the Sri Sathya Sai Institute of Higher Medical Sciences, an unparalleled institution. Bhagawan is engaged in uplifting humanity through medicine and education, both **absolutely free of cost.** Education from K.G. (Kindergarten) to P.G. (Post-Graduation) is completely free. And thousands have been treated free of charge in the departments of cardiology and urology/nephrology so far. Millions more will be helped when the departments of neurology and oncology open.

Christmas, the birthday of Jesus Christ, is the holiday of December. On December 24th, foreign devotees sing Christmas carols and bhajans for all to enjoy. Early in the morning of December 25th, the devotees sing hymns and carols by candlelight. The Avatar of our Age, dressed in sparkling white, gives *darshan* from His balcony, blessing one and all.

> What is a festive occasion ? It is when great men are born or when wicked men end their careers or vice. When virtues grow and vice is given up, man has to make it a festival.
>
> **"Sathya Sai"**

Afterword

Beloved readers of this nectar Divine.....

In all humility and earnestness, I have attempted to convey everything that I have experienced in my four decades on this Earth. Only Swami knows how long I will continue in this physical frame which is only His. **Every breath and every heartbeat of mine belong to Him alone.** At no point should anyone feel that I am a great or extraordinary person. I am only a humble servant of Bhagawan whom, in His infinite mercy, He has blessed and used as His tiny instrument in carrying out the Divine commands.

My purpose in writing this work was only to allow readers to get a glimpse into the majesty and glory of the Divine. *Never has such a loving and caring Avatar descended on this Earth.* He has given us all the chance to serve Him, to love Him, to EXPERIENCE Him. Let us not miss this golden opportunity which will never come again.

I pray to Bhagawan for His grace to continue flowing on all of us and for our Mother Earth to once again be free from the pains of Kaliyuga. May Swami's Holy name radiate and emanate from each and every human heart as only LOVE... LOVE... LOVE...

Glossary

Aarti	—	waving of burning camphor or light in front of God
Abhishekam	—	bathing
Adharma	—	unrighteousness
Ahimsa	—	non-violence
Amritha	—	Divine nectar
Ananda	—	bliss
Angavastram	—	Piece of cloth put around neck to honour someone
Atma	—	soul or inner being
Avatar	—	incarnation of God
Bal Sabha	—	students' executive body
Bangaru	—	golden; a term of affection
Beta	—	son
Beti	—	daughter
Bhabi	—	brother's wife; a term of respect
Bhaktha	—	devotee
Bhayya	—	brother
Buddhi	—	intellect
Burfi	—	an Indian sweet made from milk
Chappals	—	footwear
Darshan	—	sight of someone, usually a holy person
Dharma	—	duty; righteousness
Dhoop	—	a type of incense material
Didi	—	sister
Geeta	—	holy Hindu scripture

Gopika	—	Lord Krishna's childhood female play-mates
Guru	—	teacher; guide to spiritual liberation
Gyan	—	intellect
Japa	—	constant repetition of a name
Jhoola	—	cradle
Jija Ji	—	sister's husband
Jyoti	—	flame
Kala	—	attribute
Kama	—	sensual desires
Kangan	—	gold bracelets
Karma	—	actions
Kheer	—	a pudding made from rice, milk, and sugar
Khoya	—	a sweet made from milk
Krodha	—	anger
Leelas	—	Divine plays or miracles
Lingam	—	sacred oval shaped object representing Shiva-Shakthi
Lobha	—	greed
Lohri	—	an Indian festival
Lokas	—	worlds
Mada	—	supriority complex; pride
Maha Yogi	—	sage of the highest order
Mandir	—	temple
Mangal sutra	—	an auspicious gold ornament worn around the neck of married ladies only
Matsarya	—	jealousy

Maya	—	illusion or delusion
Moha	—	attachment
Moksha	—	liberation
Naam	—	name
Namaskar	—	reverential greeting
Navratnas	—	nine precious stones
Omkar	—	repetition of the primeval sound "Aum"
Padnamaskar	—	touching the Lotus Feet in reverance
Pad seva	—	pressing the feet
Padukas	—	slippers
Pakoda	—	a salty snack prepared by frying vegetables with a coating of gram flour
Pranams	—	to fall at someone's feet
Pranava	—	primeval sound of "Aum"
Prasad	—	eatables offered to God and then partaken by devotees
Prema	—	highest form of pure love
Puranas	—	Hindu scriptures
Rotis	—	wheat flour loaves
Sadguru	—	highest teacher; Divine teacher
Sadhaka	—	spiritual aspirant
Sadhana	—	spiritual disclipine
Sadhu	—	saint
Sakshat	—	manifest
Samadhi	—	deep meditation
Sambhashanas	—	discourse
Samithi	—	local organization of Sai devotees
Samsara	—	the world

Sankalpa	—	Divine will
Sankirtan	—	community singing of Lord's name
Sathya	—	truth
Seva	—	selfless service
Seva dal	—	one who performs selfless service
Shakthi	—	Divine energy
Shanti	—	peace
Sparshan	—	to touch
Suprabhatam	—	early morning prayers and greeting to the Lord
Tapasvi	—	a highly evolved sage
Tilak	—	vermilion mark placed on forehead
Vaikunta Dham	—	the abode of Lord Vishnu
Vedas	—	Hindu scriptures
Vedic mantras	—	hymns from Hindu scriptures
Yajnas	—	Holy fire